mer

by dimoothie

4050

Pg 128
100
107 - 124
123

free from deprivation
Don't give other power

Tab book 165

Pg 24
P 128

Free of Dieting Forever

*8 Steps to Achieve and Maintain
Your Ideal Weight*

Janet Mills

**Amber-Allen Publishing
San Rafael, California**

Amber-Allen Publishing
P.O. Box 6657
San Rafael, California 94903-0657

Library of Congress Catalog Card Number: 90-61337

First paperback edition 1990
Manufactured in the United States of America

10   9   8   7   6   5   4   3   2   1

Dedication

To have a weight problem is to suffer.
When the suffering becomes intolerable, a part of
us reaches out for answers. Finally, we come to
realize that there is a solution to the problem which
will end the suffering once and for all.

This book is dedicated to all the exasperated,
frustrated "dieters" who long
to know the truth.

Acknowledgments

I would like to acknowledge my family for their love, support and encouragement, especially my sister Dianne whose love and courage are a constant source of inspiration.

I am enormously grateful to Marc Allen for his never-ending patience, kindness and wisdom, and to Hugh Bailey, Dorothy Mills, and Harvey Dye for their generous support of this project.

Many thanks go to Katherine Hendon, Gail Austin, and Susannah Baldwin for their editing assistance, and to Bonnie Smetts for designing the cover.

And finally, I'd like to extend a warm thank you to Pamala Oslie and Steven Kahn for bringing light into my life just when I needed it.

Contents

Part I

Free of Dieting Forever

Part II

The Way Toward Permanent Weight Loss

Part III

Recognizing Where You Are Now . . . and What You Have Been Doing

Part IV

Knowing Where You Want to Go . . . and Understanding Why

Part V

How You Will Get There

Part VI

8 Steps to Achieve and Maintain Your Ideal Weight

ACTION GUIDE

Tools and Techniques
to Apply Your Power Constructively

Note to the reader

The information contained in this book is not intended to replace the advice of a medical professional, especially for those who are obese, have eating disorders, or a serious health condition such as diabetes. This book is sold with the understanding that the publisher and author are not engaged in rendering medical or professional advice. The author and Amber-Allen Publishing shall have neither liability nor responsibility to any person or entity with respect to any loss or damage caused or alleged to be caused directly or indirectly by the information contained in this book.

Preface

If frustration and despair have become your constant companions, perhaps it is time to ask why.

You were not born into this world to be miserable. In fact, all misery is simply a misunderstanding and mis-direction of creative energy. With knowledge and understanding you can redirect your energy toward a new way of thinking, feeling, and doing. You can learn to use the powers of your mind, emotions and body to free yourself of excess weight—without conscious struggle and striving, without dieting, without pills, without pain.

Once you are willing to open your mind, ask yourself questions, and expect to find answers, you will find them. But instead of questioning, "Why me? Why must I deal with a perpetual weight problem?" you might ask, "What is this problem trying to teach me? How can I learn from this situation?"

These latter questions will lead you back to your "self." In your search for self-understanding, you may begin to realize the part you play in forming your life as well as the shape of your body. And as you take responsibility for your actions, you may come to know that you are blessed with free will and unlimited powers of creativity that await your recognition and use.

The purpose of this book is to expand your awareness of the power you have to change your body and to remind you of the universal principles operating in your life. It will serve as an introduction to concepts that can change your life, but by no means is it the final word on the subject.

If it moves your mind out of its customary and comfortable patterns of thinking, and attunes it to new possibilities for constructive action, then it will have served its purpose.

This book is my gift to you, to each of you with questions like I once had—still longing for answers. May it inspire and guide you to the joyful experience of achieving and maintaining your ideal weight and free you from dieting forever.

Introduction

What you are about to learn is a philosophy toward life, toward your "self" and your body.

It is a permanent approach toward weight loss that considers the condition of your mind and emotions as well as your body. It touches upon the more complete picture of *who* you are, *why* you are this way and *what* you can do about it.

It is not about dieting, exercise plans or rigid weight loss programs of any sort. You won't be asked to take pills or vitamins, eat certain foods and give up others, weigh your food, or even weigh yourself. Actually, this approach to weight loss is the opposite of dieting in many ways. You don't have to give up anything, resist your favorite foods or control your behavior through avoidance tactics. You will learn why these actions don't work and what to do instead.

To be free of dieting forever is to find a way of looking at yourself and your body from a new perspective. It is about having, gaining, and accepting what you want from life instead of losing, giving up, or getting rid of what you don't want. More importantly, it is a process of healing and inner change that comes about through the discovery and release of your inner power and potential.

The 8 Steps are powerful principles that will help you to focus and direct the powers of your mind, emotions, and body toward constructive change that will bring you what you want. As you apply these principles, nothing can stop you from achieving and maintaining your ideal weight, or from having almost anything and everything your heart desires.

How To Use This Book

This book is designed to help you clarify your desires and make some very important decisions in your life. It asks questions; please take time to answer them. Within your answers are the keys that will "unlock your problem" and set you free.

To receive the greatest benefit from ideas presented in this book, you may want to read the entire book once (without stopping to answer the questions) and then read it again more slowly a second time. As you read it a second time, make an effort to become actively involved with the ideas and information as they are presented.

Record your thoughts, feelings, and responses to questions in a separate notebook or journal. (Ruled paper that you can store in a binder later on will do just fine.) Give yourself plenty of time to completely absorb the meaning and energy behind the ideas and to respond to each of the questions.

When you come across thoughts, suggestions, and techniques that appeal to you, jot them down or note the page number in your journal. In addition to providing a place to record book notes, a separate notebook or binder can serve as a private journal for recording your own ideas and insights.

This book contains a series of key concepts that you will want to remember and refer to again and again. These are printed in large, italicized text. There are also a number of "power words" that play a significant part in your understanding of the concepts (and thus your success). The power words are often printed in bold type for emphasis.

In the Action Guide is a glossary of the power words that will clarify their meaning and provide an opportunity for you to carefully consider the "power" behind each word. You may want to refer to the glossary as each power word appears or review the entire list of words before you read this book a second time.

Use this book as a tool. Think of it as a workbook and guide toward learning and understanding what you must do to achieve your ideal weight. Give yourself permission to write in it, highlight text, or mark in it for future reference.

Repetition is the key to learning; thus many of the key concepts and The 8 Steps are intentionally repeated throughout the text, as well as summarized in later chapters. For a while, you will need to continually reinforce your new habits of thinking until they take root and have the strength to stand on their own.

Don't expect to apply every idea (especially the 8 Steps) all at once. It is better to focus on one concept at a time. Gradually, as you apply an idea toward constructive change in your life, you will find that it becomes second nature to you. Over a period of time, quite without your conscious notice, many of the key concepts will become your own.

For many years I was overweight, on a diet, and very miserable about it. Throughout those years I never stopped searching for solutions to my "fat problem." I wanted to know why I wasn't able to lose weight and keep it off even though I made numerous attempts to do so.

Today I am no longer burdened by a fat problem and I feel satisfied with the answers I have found. In fact, I have wanted to write this book in order to summarize these answers as much for myself as I have for others. I am still learning to apply them in other areas of my life!

The ideas presented in this book will give you much to think about ("food for thought") and lead you to a better understanding and acceptance of the truth about permanent weight loss. One solid idea may be all it takes to transform your life from misery and despair to joy and relief from the burden of your weight problem. Yet this book offers many ideas that you may have overlooked in your search for a solution.

Of course, ideas can do nothing for you until you put them to use, so be sure to read the section entitled "Action Guide: Tools and Techniques to Apply Your Power Constructively." This part of the book offers specific actions you can take right away toward becoming the person you want to be.

Inner change will take place only when there is a readiness and willingness to change. No one can force you to accept ideas that you aren't ready to hear about. If you will begin with an open mind and an eagerness to learn, you will get much more from this book. The most important thing is to go out and do it: apply what you learn, and with patience, practice, and perseverance you will undoubtedly succeed.

Part I

Free of Dieting Forever

There is no such thing as a problem without a gift for you in its hands. You seek problems because you need their gifts.

--Richard Bach

Chapter 1

My Fat Story

I know what it's like to be fat. I spent many long years of my life living in a body three sizes larger than I wanted it to be.

But my problem was not merely excess weight. After endless attempts and failures to lose weight by dieting, I was filled with a dreadful fear that I would *stay* fat forever.

The fear and frustration of not knowing how to overcome my problem eventually threatened my mental and physical health, my social life and my career. I lost confidence and self-respect, and hated myself for lacking the discipline and self-control I believed was necessary to lose weight and keep it off.

Eating to Live, Living to Eat

I hadn't always suffered from a fat problem. During my childhood and early twenties, I considered eating a necessary function—not the focal point of my life. I would eat whatever I wanted to eat, whenever I was hungry, and never thought much about it.

In college I was always on the go with very little time to eat at all. I would skip breakfast and eat candy bars and snacks from vending machines between classes; cooking something wholesome and nutritious was simply out of the question. As far as I was concerned, eating was a nuisance I could do without.

I would never have imagined that I could gain so much weight and lose control of my eating habits, but that is precisely what happened. Years later, I found myself at the opposite end of the scale, compulsively stuffing my body with food, looking forward to every meal, and craving all types of "fattening" foods.

After college, I moved to California and became more aware of nutrition and its effect on my health and well-being. Since I had abused my body for years, I felt it was time to eat wholesome, natural foods such as raw cashews, dried fruit, homemade whole wheat bread, and cookies filled with sunflower seeds, raisins, and carob chips. I also indulged in a variety of foods that I had never enjoyed before such as avocados and Mexican food.

It all began quite innocently. I wasn't concerned about the gradual weight gain, although my jeans were getting tighter and the top snap was popping open every time I sat down. Whenever I went out to eat, I would unbutton my skirt or loosen the zipper on my pants to be comfortable. Of course, I had to select blouses and seating arrangements to carefully conceal this habit of mine.

Then my sister from New Jersey came to see me. Two years had passed since our last visit, and she expected to see the same slender, petite body she had always known. The full figure and fat face that greeted her at the airport was quite a shock, and she didn't hesitate to tell me so. My friends hadn't mentioned that I looked a lot heavier; I never realized that my fat was so obvious to others. As far as I was concerned, I was doing a great job concealing it.

Time to Go on a Diet

Almost suddenly, I became aware of my "fat problem." I decided it was time to *lose weight* and, of course, the thing to do (that is, what most people do in a situation like this) is *go on a diet*. Since I had enjoyed a "normal" weight all of my life, it would be a quick and simple task to lose the extra pounds.

At least the origin of my particular fat problem could be traced back to the previous year. I couldn't blame my weight gain on heredity or an underactive thyroid. I knew my problem was entirely self-induced by overeating. And the solution seemed simple enough: cut out excess calories, give up all "fattening" foods, increase my exercise, and the weight would melt away, fast and easy.

I wasn't interested in fad diets, the "lose-5-pounds-in-one-week" type. I simply began to consider ways of cutting calories from my diet, prescribing to myself what I could and could not eat. Bread and butter were the first offenders to go, along with chocolate and anything with a lot of sugar in it. Unfortunately, my favorite foods are bread, chocolate, pasta, and starches of any kind, so this is when the *real* problem began.

A Slave to Food

The more I endeavored to avoid certain foods, the more I craved them; and it wasn't long before they gained a lot of "power" over me. Whenever I'd make the mistake of giving in to a piece of chocolate, the guilt I suffered afterward was awful—not to mention the fear of gaining five pounds from eating it! I would devour almost an entire box of wheat crackers as if my life depended on it, and then mope around for the remainder of the week in remorse for my transgressions.

I felt like—and actually became—a slave to food. Food developed an incredible attraction to me and I to it. I became trapped in a vicious circle of binging followed by guilt, disappointment, and deprivation. I would continually count calories, and sometimes succeed in eating "light" for a day or two, maybe even a week at a time, but then I'd always give in to the urge to eat. Sooner or later, I was out of control again and my diet was blown to bits.

I was so disgusted with myself for starting each new diet with great enthusiasm, only to give up or fail to reach my goal, again and again.

"Fat Clothes" and Broken Zippers

As the months went by, I grew beyond pleasantly plump ("cherubic" as someone once described me) and my once casual concern was rapidly turning into a frantic haste to get rid of the extra weight. I didn't appreciate being called a cherub, nor could I afford to buy entire sets of clothing two, three, and four sizes larger than I had ever worn. Since I had grown in stages—not all at once—I had to acquire clothes to fit me at each stage of my growth.

My wardrobe evolved into a mish-mash of what I called "fat clothes." These were carefully selected items of clothing whose primary function was to conceal the bulges of fat hanging over the waistline of my pants. Actually, they allowed me to hide the fact that most of the time my pants were completely open, making it easier for me to breathe and bend over. I stopped wearing blouses tucked in, and gave up wearing belts because they were always hidden under a large maternity-type blouse anyway. My clothes suffered with me: I split seams, broke dozens of zippers, popped more buttons from my blouses and pants than I care to remember, but kept right on eating and mending.

Then my sister came to California for a second visit, took one look at me and gasped, "Oh, you look awful, you've got to do something!" If she only knew how hard I'd been trying! Feelings of anxiety and frustration were increasing by the moment. I realized if my sister couldn't stand to see me in my present condition, my problem was serious. This time, I suppose she wasn't accustomed to seeing me with a double chin.

Searching for Answers Outside Myself

For years I truly believed there was an answer *out there* somewhere. I knew there had to be a solution to my problem, but I just couldn't figure it out. Many times I prayed for the answer, hoping to receive a revelation or clear understanding of what I was doing wrong and how to do it right.

It wasn't that I lacked determination to overcome my fat problem. I made every attempt to understand precisely *what* emotional problem was underlying my indulgences, and *why* I had managed to gain so much weight. I constantly made plans regarding what, when and how I was going to do something about it.

I read every book and magazine article about dieting, exercise and nutrition I could get my hands on. Standing in the check-out lines of the supermarket, I would scan all the magazines for the latest miracle fad diets promising weight loss of five, ten or fifteen pounds in a week. I attended every adult education class and seminar I could possibly fit into my schedule, hoping to find the answer to my problem.

I kept thinking I'd discover a new method, some particular technique or concept, that would work for me. I tried non-prescription diet capsules loaded with caffeine to suppress my appetite, dietary candy, fasting for three days at a time, fruit juice diets, vegetable diets, meatless diets, water-melon-only-for-one-week diets, high protein diets—you name it, and I probably tried it. I lost weight on most of these programs, only to *gain it all back again* as soon as I resumed eating in the manner I had become accustomed to and enjoyed.

During this time, I also maintained a vigorous exercise program, running and walking and doing calisthenics twice a day. This did help me to appear thinner because of increased muscle tone, but my weight on the scale would not budge. In fact, many times it went up even though I was sticking to my diet and doing my exercise. That was truly one of the most frustrating and humiliating experiences!

I became so discouraged, so completely exasperated and tired of struggling with this problem. Every day I would pray to God, *"Please help me!"* I could not stand myself any longer. Every single moment of my life, I was aware of the feeling that I was carrying a terrible burden, a need to overcome something within myself that I could not quite identify, understand or tolerate for one more day.

A Happy Ending

It took me several years to discover what I had been doing wrong, and to realize that dieting doesn't work. Well, it does work if you want to be on a diet for the rest of your life. But personally, I could not stand the thought of dieting forever. I wanted to eat what I enjoy eating, when I wanted it, and I also wanted to be thin.

For a time, I actually believed I couldn't "have my cake and eat it too." I believed I would have to give up one or the other: all of my favorite foods, or a thin, attractive body. Yet eventually I *did* lose all my excess weight and I *didn't* gain it back.

To my surprise, an even greater benefit resulted from my struggle with food, fat and fear: I learned some very important principles about the nature of my "self" and my body. That awful experience led me to understand how I was responsible for creating and maintaining the physical appearance I was so unhappy with.

I began to realize a few things about weight loss that I had never read or heard about before. I discovered that maintaining one's ideal weight will come naturally when some basic changes are made in the way we think and feel about ourself and our body.

I decided to organize my ideas, along with the best ideas I had learned from others, into a series of key concepts and 8 powerful steps to be used as a guideline for losing weight and keeping it off.

This book is a synthesis of some of the most practical ideas and techniques that I've learned about in my personal experience and studies. None of the ideas are new. In fact, many of them have been around for centuries. Though times may change and words may change, certain truths remain constant.

Part II

The Way Toward Permanent Weight Loss

Life is a journey, not a destination.

--Author Unknown

Chapter 2

What Must You Do to Achieve Your Ideal Weight?

There are only so many things you *can* do to create a change in the shape and condition of your body.You can **think** differently, **feel** differently and **act** differently.

You know by now that losing weight permanently will mean doing something different than you have done so far. There must be something you have overlooked, since you've tried so many times before and have failed to achieve or maintain your ideal weight.

What you may have overlooked is this:

I*t is not just what you do to
your body that counts,
but what you believe about yourself
and your body . . .
what you think and feel and
expect to achieve while you
are doing it.*

Your **thoughts, feelings,** and **expectations** act as the motivating power to propel you into some action or behavior. It isn't possible for you to eat or overeat without a thought to direct that activity. Every action you take is preceded by a thought or inner feeling-image that provides the impulse and direction for action to follow.

Ultimately the condition of your body *is* affected by the actions you take each day—what you eat, how much you eat, and how often—yet those actions must originate within your mind.

T*his is why the only way to
lose weight permanently, without
ever dieting again, is to change the
inner images held within your mind:
the beliefs, thoughts, and feelings
you have about yourself
and your body.*

Your inner state of mind affects your appetite, your energy level, and every outer condition you experience in life. You can starve your body until it's little more than skin and bones, but if you fail to change the inner beliefs, thoughts, and feelings responsible for generating your actions, you will gain the weight right back again.

To achieve and maintain your ideal weight, you must begin to question the ideas you take for granted about yourself and your body. You must examine your beliefs about food and weight loss. Your habitual thoughts will follow the pattern of your beliefs, your predominant feelings will follow your thoughts, and what you do with your body follows all of these.

Changing Who You Are On The Inside

In order to lose your excess weight forever, you must be willing to gain new ideas and insight about yourself and your body. For instance, you may think of your problem as a need to "lose weight" and focus on the discrepancy between the way you look now and the way you want to look. Yet the challenge you truly need to address is the difference between *who* you are now and who you want to become.

It may sound trivial, but the difference in how you perceive your problem is important. Deciding to change "who you are" includes your inner thoughts and feelings, while "what you look like" or "losing weight" merely focuses your attention on the outer effect of your thoughts and feelings.

Who you are includes your beliefs about the nature of yourself, your body, and food. Who you are is what you think about, how you feel, and what you do with your mental, emotional, and physical energy every hour, day after day.

When your attention is constantly focused on food, fat, and the current shape of your body, it's easy to forget that the *cause* of your problem begins with those inner thoughts and images! And it's the cause, not the effect that must be dealt with.

Y*ou can achieve your ideal weight.*
You can have a body that
reflects who you want to be
just as soon as you are ready and
willing to be that person
in thought, in feeling, and in action.

Again, the change must first take place with who you are on the inside. This means being someone who thinks and feels and acts differently than you presently do. It means "letting go" of your constant attention to the problem and acting *as if* you are the person you want to be right now instead of wishing you could be "someday."

You can become the person you want to be by deciding to focus your attention upon your strengths instead of your weaknesses, upon your objectives instead of the obstacles that stand in your way, upon your own unique attributes of beauty instead of each tiny flaw. Soon these inner changes will be reflected without, in your actions, and in the health and condition of your body.

You Know Where You Want to Go, But Don't Know How to Get There

Perhaps you realize that changing your outer appearance will require a change in the pattern of your inner beliefs, thoughts, and feelings. You may be convinced that you need to change who you are on the inside and become your "ideal image" in your mind . . . but how do you do it? Where do you begin?

What you need is a course of action to follow, one you can absolutely trust to take you where you want to go.

Look at it this way: creating a positive change in the inner image of yourself is like preparing to take a journey. Journeys require effort—not only physical effort, but mental preparation, emotional commitment, and faith that you will reach your destination.

In fact, if you stop to think about it, almost anything you do requires effort on each of these levels. Without the **desire** to take a journey, you will never set foot in a distant land. If you merely dream about faraway places, without **believing** it's possible for you to be there, you won't ever make the necessary **decisions** and arrangements for getting there.

If you believe you can go, do everything required on the mental level, but fail to take the first physical step out the door, you won't get very far either. You could be on your way, but if you lose all your enthusiasm for going, you might change your mind and stay at home.

Whether your desire is to change your appearance or to move from one point on the globe to another . . .

*To be effective, action must be taken
on every level of your ability
to take action.*

Mental action — Through desire, intent, purpose, imagination and planning.

Emotional action — Through decision or commitment, expectation, enthusiasm, faith, or belief in your desire.

Physical action — Through a willingness to back up your desire and decision with action. By following through on your intuitive impulses to act.

These are actions you take all the time to accomplish the most simple task, so there is nothing you need to learn *how* to do. If you can plan a trip and follow through with your plan, you have everything you need to solve your "weight problem."

Just be willing to keep an open mind. **Believe** that you can solve this problem like any other, then act on this belief, just as you are doing in other areas of your life. **Trust** that the power and potential to achieve your desire is within you right now and **decide** that you will apply your power constructively.

Chapter 3

How Do You Apply Your Power Constructively?

Imagine for a moment, that you want to take a trip to Hawaii. If you are sitting in your living room in Poughkeepsie, New York you are going to have to *do* something to get you there. What would you be thinking and how would you be feeling if you were ready to take a vacation? What must you believe in order to achieve this desire?

First of all, the vacation promises to provide sensations, feelings and personal *rewards* that you want or need to experience. You might begin to picture yourself in Hawaii *right now*. Perhaps you see and feel yourself lying on the beach, basking in the sun, or enjoying the sights, scents, and surroundings of a tropical environment. In your imagination it feels wonderful, and you are inspired to do it.

You **decide** upon a definite time to go. Reservations are made with an airline and hotel because you fully intend to be there. You **expect** to have a good time and enjoy yourself or why bother to spend all this money? You have **faith** that the airline you choose will get you there. If you didn't **trust** the transportation—airplane, ship or auto—you certainly wouldn't get very far.

If you were to concentrate solely on how miserable you are at the moment, would you ever take the first step out the door? It isn't likely. Or if you were to focus on all the obstacles that can stand in your way, would you even want to go? Probably not. The plane may crash, the airlines might lose your luggage (they lost mine), it may rain the entire time you are there (it happens), you may suffer from a terrible sunburn on your first day at the beach. The list of potential mishaps is endless, but normally you don't think of these things or *dwell* on them because if you **believe** they will happen, you will stay right where you are.

> Y*our thoughts must motivate you*
> *toward effective action. The type*
> *of feelings that accompany your*
> *thoughts must be enthusiastic, filled*
> *with faith, expectation, and*
> *anticipation of reward.*

Therefore, your **beliefs** about yourself must generate constructive thought. They must tell you that you deserve (are worthy of) the rewards that this vacation promises, that you have or will somehow find everything you need to get you there. Your beliefs must enable you to trust that you will reach your destination and eventually experience the wonderful feelings you anticipate.

Now **imagine** that you are embarking upon an inner journey. Consider where you are now (who you are and how you look) as Point A and your destination (who you want to become and how you want to look) as Point Z. Form a clear picture in your mind of the entire experience of being there.

Imagine how you will think and feel and act. Imagine how your body will feel when you are living your life at Point Z. This is extremely important. Without a clear **decision** about where you want to go it is impossible to get there!

On the following page are some questions you might ask yourself as you prepare for a journey. The kind of questions you would ask as you plan a vacation are relevant to your inner journey from Point A to Z.

Take ten minutes right now to consider your answers to these questions. Then write your response to these questions in your notebook or journal.

YOUR VACATION	YOUR INNER JOURNEY
Where do I want to go?	Who do I want to become?
How will I get there?	How will I become this person?
What is the most direct route, because I'm anxious to be there?	What is the most efficient way for me to achieve my ideal weight?
When will I arrive?	When can I expect to achieve it?
Why do I want to go there anyway?	Do I really want to change and become a different person, or is it someone else's idea of the way I should be?
What will I do there?	What do I expect to enjoy or accomplish by making this change?
What will the weather be like?	How will it feel when I finally arrive?
What will it cost?	Is it truly worth the effort? Am I willing to expend the energy it will take to get there?
Who's coming with me?	Who's on my side? Will my friends and family welcome and support my new image?

Until you have honestly addressed these issues, you won't know whether you're serious about going anywhere, about changing who you are. Even if you think you know the answers to these questions, it will help to write them down and see them in black and white. The point of this exercise is to clarify your **desire** and to evaluate your **commitment** to achieve it.

The distance between Point A and Point Z represents the mental, emotional and physical actions you must take to achieve your ideal weight. Can you **imagine** yourself taking the necessary steps and finally arriving at Point Z? Or do you doubt that you have what it takes to make this trip—that the distance is far beyond your reach?

Within your answers to these questions are clues to understanding why you have failed to arrive at Point Z. For instance, you may find that you don't really know where you want to go, that is, precisely *who* you want to become or what you can realistically expect to look like. Or maybe you do know where you want to go, but don't **believe** you'll ever get there.

Perhaps you expect to arrive at your destination in two weeks when it's actually a six-month trip. Or you have tried taking too many shortcuts that bring you right back where you started from. Maybe you don't really want to go, but others think you should and expect you to.

Think about it! You are the one who must **feel** inspired to do it. YOU must feel enthusiastic about taking this journey and **expect** to get there, or you never will.

Getting Started

Remember what you thought and how you felt while planning your imaginary trip to Hawaii? So it is with creating a new image for yourself. You must be prepared to *do* whatever it takes to accomplish your objective. You must be behind the idea all the way, with all of your energy and enthusiasm. It is up to you to **decide** where you want to go, **commit** to a clear plan of action and **believe** that you have (or will find) the means to get there.

With a clear **desire** to move your "self" from Point A to Point Z, you begin to **imagine** being there right now. You begin to see and **feel** yourself looking the way you want to look, enjoying all the sensations that accompany this thought. You must make a **commitment** to be there and then confidently **expect** that you will become the person you desire to be.

In your imagination, capture the **feeling** of how wonderful it is to be there and forget about the obstacles that might stand in your way. This is not to say you can't be aware of obstacles, but it isn't necessary to dwell on them until they deplete the energy of your enthusiasm and desire.

Really, the only major obstacle that can prevent you from reaching your destination is *you*. Yet, when you have a clear desire to become the person you want to be and make up your mind to do it, even *you* will no longer threaten or sabotage your success.

Since the day you were born, you have directed your imagination, emotions and body toward the achievement of goals in every facet of your life. Again, it is desire, intent and purpose, carried by the energy of enthusiasm and expectation and backed by effective action, that will move you toward your ideal body weight.

This may sound difficult if you are feeling fat and frustrated, but notice the way you accomplish *anything* you want to do and you will realize how effortlessly you apply your energy toward constructive activity all the time.

M*ost of us are simply not in the habit of treating a weight problem the way we do other*

challenges in our lives.
Instead, we have the habit of focusing
on the obstacles that might stand
in our way. We imagine all the
reasons why we will fail to arrive at
our destination, instead of
envisioning what it's like to BE there.

Because we focus on the obstacles, we experience all the negative emotions associated with them. We feel anxious, threatened, powerless and frustrated, instead of confident, enthusiastic and expectant of success.

Once you are stuck in this kind of emotional rut—a repetitive pattern of self-destructive thoughts, feelings and actions—you need to step up your energy through desire and decision, pull yourself out and move forward. It requires persistent use of your imagination and emotions toward your purpose and intent (having a more slender body) not toward what you fear may happen (failing to achieve it).

Your non-constructive habits of thought and feeling can be replaced just as soon as you truly **desire** and **decide** to replace them. Once you do, it won't be long before you are enjoying the results you have been dreaming of.

Chapter 4

Beyond Dieting: The Journey Begins

For years I searched for the diet that would work for me. It never occurred to me that I might lose weight by going off my diet and doing the opposite of what I believed was necessary to lose weight.

Because I believed, as many of the diet books and schemes will tell you, that losing weight is simply a matter of burning more calories than you consume, my failure to accomplish this feat became *my* fault. Obviously it wasn't the diet's fault. There had to be some character flaw (perhaps a deep-seated neurosis) or serious problem with me, not the methods, because I tried them all!

Diets do work as long as you stay on them. In fact, almost any diet will work like a charm if you follow it to the letter and have the self-discipline to stick with it for at least five to thirty days. The question is, what are you supposed to do after that? Are you supposed to be so thrilled with your new body that bread and butter or a chocolate fudge sundae won't tempt you any longer?

A simple measure of success is when you decide to do something, and then do it. Eventually you stop trying to lose (or maintain) your weight by dieting, and inevitably you become a "failure" in your own eyes. The result is a further loss of self-esteem, which only serves to magnify and perpetuate a weight problem.

Without a true **desire** and **decision** to stick with a diet, you will half-heartedly "try" and whole-heartedly fail. You lose weight, gain it back again, and eventually feel very disappointed in yourself for failing to accomplish what you set out to do with such initial, but short-lived, enthusiasm.

Once you are lost in a maze of fat-related problems and don't know which way to turn, it can be difficult to see the whole picture. What I failed to see years ago (and what I now know with certainty), is that merely going on a diet will not solve a weight problem. Yet for me, dieting was the only way someone could possibly expect to lose weight. A desire to lose weight and the need to go on a diet were synonymous, like two sides of an equation.

If you have been on a perpetual diet for more years than you care to remember (or on and off one) and still haven't achieved your desired weight, maybe its time to consider this: It isn't your fault for failing again and again to lose weight by dieting. It is simply that the *method* you have chosen has some serious flaws in it.

Perhaps you have also mistakenly assumed that going on a diet was your only option. The assumption that dieting is the answer to losing weight is a prevalent part of Western culture. Yet, if simply following a diet plan was truly an effective means of losing weight and keeping it off, there wouldn't be so many of them. Surely two or three of the best known diets would work for almost anyone—if they worked at all. Yet the reason why new ideas for diets pop up everyday is because dieters need new diets to keep them going after the old ones fail to bring them satisfaction or a slender body.

There is Another Way to Get There

If you were traveling in your car toward your destination and your radiator developed a leak, how would you choose to deal with this problem? Would you keep filling it with water every time your engine overheated, or would you decide to find the crack and fix it for good? If you're in a big hurry, you will probably just add water. But that's a temporary solution, and so are dieting, deprivation or starvation.

Sooner or later you will accept the fact that you must locate the crack in your radiator and fix it because you'll get bored with the task of filling it up. Eventually, you must also accept the fact that there is a crack in the logic of dieting as the only solution to your problem, and your habitual behavior is bound to seep through all your heroic attempts to stop it.

You may define your problem as the need to lose weight, and think the only way to do it is to go on a diet. You may look at the physical evidence—too much fat—and believe the only way to reduce fat is to reduce the calories you consume. These ideas are based upon the false belief that the body is merely a physical mechanism (similar to a computer: "garbage in—garbage out") without any intimate relationship to the state of your mind and emotions.

E*xcess fat is not just on the physical*
level in the form of calories and
fat cells; it exists as a reflection of the
inner image of your self,
the inner image of your body,
and the anxious,"dis-eased" state
of your emotions.

Diets so often fail to consider your emotional state or much more than counting calories, that it's no wonder dieters are endlessly frustrated and in search of a better idea. What is needed is a comprehensive approach to the problem of weight loss, one that endeavors to achieve a balance and greater harmony between the mind, emotions, and body.

Of course, there is nothing wrong with going on a diet if you want to and it feels like the right thing to do. Dieting will speed up your progress especially when you **believe** that it will, and are **committed** to following through with it for a given period of time. No diet, however, should be taken very seriously unless your physician prescribes it for medical reasons.

Without the proper mental attitude, diets are hazardous to your emotional health because they promise so much and deliver so little. Too often they keep your mind focused on the symptoms of your problem instead of relieving the cause, and this keeps your emotions in a constant state of anxiety and frustration.

Instead of dwelling upon the little grains of sand in your shoe (like food, fat, and failure) why not look at the larger picture of your life? You are a powerful person with all the potential you will ever need to move your mind beyond the limited scope of your present situation. You can become even stronger in power and greater in purpose.

All you need is a willingness to open your mind and see a larger vision of your life, to realize that there is so much more than food and fat that can capture your attention and bring you the inner fulfillment and satisfaction you desire.

What's more important than sticking to a diet is learning how to **accept** yourself as you are, to **love** yourself and **forgive** yourself for being who you are at the moment, even if it's not who you want to be. It is more important that you learn how to relax your anxious thoughts about food and fat than to strive or struggle to consciously control them.

Instead of resisting your favorite foods, you can decide to moderate the amount of food you eat or eat only those foods you crave for a day. The next day it will be highly unlikely that you still crave them. As you let go of your need to control what, when and how much you eat, you free a great deal of mental, emotional and physical energy that can be directed elsewhere.

Instead of going on another diet, take the time to understand the cause of your problem. The cause is in the way you think and feel about yourself and your body, which naturally leads you to act the way you do.

Your Inner Wisdom

The human mind and body are complex miracles of creative energy. Therefore, when it comes to a matter that no one but an all-knowing God could know about for sure, you must learn to trust the wisdom of your own inner self.

The wisdom of your inner self (or subconscious mind) regulates every vital function of your body. There is no doubt that it can regulate your appetite and maintain the weight that is ideal for you, if you allow it to, **expect** it to, and **trust** that it will.

U*se the power of your conscious mind to clarify your desire and commit to achieve it. Then allow the power of your subconscious mind to accomplish the task for you— efficiently and effortlessly with its ancient, infallible wisdom.*

There is a solution to every problem. The answers to your problem will come to you when you ask for them and **expect** them to. They will come from your own inner guidance or inner voice of intuition. You simply need to become clear about what you want to know, ask for guidance, and then listen.

The answer may come to you in the form of an urge or an impulse to take some action. However small or seemingly insignificant, **trust** that each action you take is bringing you closer to your desire.

Your inner self will find the best way of guiding you toward your desire. When you trust the inner wisdom of your intuition to guide you, you know you can't go wrong. In fact, there is no need to judge any decision you make as right or wrong once you realize that you have the power to make the best of that decision.

To maintain your ideal weight
without dieting, you must
abandon your conscious control
of what you eat and form
the habit of listening to your
body for inner messages of hunger
instead of outer signals that
it's time to eat.

This will allow a natural relationship with food to develop—one that is regulated and maintained by your subconscious mind.

Once you release your desire to the power of your subconscious mind, you don't need to be concerned with how you will achieve it. Your main concern is to break the habit of struggling and striving, learn to relax and **trust** your inner power to guide you. Trust this part of yourself, and you will draw upon your innate ability to go wherever you want to go and be whomever you want to be.

The Journey Begins

Right now, you are about to take one of the most important journeys of your life. It is a journey inside yourself to discover who you really are, what you truly desire to accomplish, why you have failed before, and what you can do to reach your destination.

You are the captain of this journey, and everything you need for success is already within you. There's no need to struggle or strive to get anywhere, you only need to discover and reveal what has been there all along.

As you journey from "who you are now" to "who you want to become," take time to reflect on any truth that becomes apparent to you, especially if you are seeing it for the first time. Remember to record your thoughts, feelings and experiences in a private notebook or journal. One day you may want to look at these to see how far you have traveled.

The next four sections of this book will help you gain further insight into yourself and your situation. They are aimed at encouraging you to look at your situation from a different point of view. As you view your situation from a new perspective, your heightened understanding will lift you above your present emotional attachment to your problem, bringing you many steps closer to success.

Just be willing to release a few of your old ideas and to embrace the new that feel right to you. A single idea could lead you to victory over the challenge that lies before you.

The Journey — At a glance

Recognizing Where You Are Now . . .

Who you are now (Point A). Your beliefs, thoughts, feelings and expectations about your self, your body and food.　*. . . and What You Have Been Doing*

Your over-all attitude and the typical actions you have taken to create a change in the shape of your body.

Knowing Where You Want to Go . . .

Who you want to become (Point Z). The kind of thoughts, feelings and actions you expect to experience once you have reached your ideal weight.

. . . and Understanding Why

What truly motivates you to change. Understanding the real reasons for "losing weight."

How You Will Get There

Preliminary actions you can take to "break up" your current habits of thought, feeling and action.

8 Steps to Achieve and MaintainYour Ideal Weight

A summary of powerful principles for creating new patterns of thought, feeling and action. Steps that will lead you toward your ideal weight and the *only* ones that will enable you to maintain it.

Chapter 5

Your Inner Dialogue:
Habitual Thoughts
and Feelings

Begin by considering where you are right now, not your physical condition, how much weight you need to lose, but the condition of your mind and your emotions. Imagine for a moment that you are stepping outside of yourself to view your personal world from "above."

If you could observe your behavior throughout a typical week, you would undoubtedly begin to notice certain habits and routines that you engage in every day. You have your own way of doing things, whether it's getting ready to go to work, preparing a meal, or brushing your teeth. But it's not this kind of habit that you need to become aware of. Many habits are useful for saving time and thought-energy. Because you don't have to think about how to shower, brush your teeth, drive your car, or make a cup of coffee every time you do it, your mind is free to wander and think about other things.

So what *are* you thinking about while you go through your daily routines, and what kind of feelings accompany these thoughts?

Most of us have the habit of thinking the same type of thoughts while absorbed in our routine behavior. And it is this kind of habit that you need to become aware of.
It is this kind of habit that often robs you not only of your enjoyment of the moment, but of the kind of life you wish to live and the type of body you want to have.

What do you think about while you're getting dressed in the morning? Perhaps you like to use this time to plan your day or to contemplate what to eat for breakfast. Maybe you like to sing light-heartedly as you shower or think of what you should have said during an argument with your spouse the day before. Does your mind tend to wander toward images of a feast of food spread out before you?

Maybe you have the habit of looking in the mirror while you dress. If so, are you also in the habit of uttering strong words of self-contempt as you struggle to squeeze your body into your clothes?

Continue to imagine that you are viewing yourself from "above" while you move throughout a typical day. Listen very carefully for the typical and repetitive comments you make out loud. What do you hear yourself saying? Notice what you say to yourself as well as the comments you make to others.

Are you having any trouble doing this? Perhaps it will help if I describe some of my own thoughts during my fat days. I can tell you precisely what I used to think about because I kept a journal of my thoughts and feelings.

Back to "My Fat Story"

When I was overweight, the state of my mind and emotions was one of desperation and frustration— desperation because I couldn't stand being fat anymore; frustration because I didn't know what to do about it. My typical thoughts and the feelings that accompanied them were like an inner battleground: a frightening conflict filled with mass confusion and despair.

Eating had become a full-time occupation and literally consumed most of my waking thoughts throughout the day. What to eat, when to eat, whether to eat, how much to eat, and finally, why did I eat that at all? The inner dialogue went something like this:

What should I eat today?
> (or What shouldn't I eat?)

Just for today, I'm going to think thin and eat
light meals.
> (Can I do it?)

I'm really going to do it this time.
> (I hope . . .)

I've got to stick to my diet.
> (Sure you will . . .)

How many pounds can I lose this week?
> (Try to be realistic . . .)

I'm going to lose five pounds by Friday if it
kills me.
> (It just might . . .)

I've got to stop eating bread this week and eat
more salads.
> (Oh no, I hate to eat salads without
> bread . . .)

In the midst of these misdirected attempts to control my eating habits, there was still another side of me that looked forward with great anticipation to every meal and chocolate morsel I'd allow myself to indulge in. Repeatedly I'd say to myself, "Why can't I lose this weight?" "What is my *problem?*" Then a moment later a voice inside me would urge me on, telling me to "go ahead and eat what you want, you can run it off tomorrow . . . eat, eat!"

Apparently, my desire to be slender was equally as strong as my desire to eat, and the conflict raged on. In competition with the voice inside giving me the go ahead was a type of thought which warned me to stop. "Stop being such a pig!" "Stop, or you'll have to start all over again!" "Please, stick with your diet this time!" But for me, losing weight by going on a diet was impossible—except, of course, on a temporary basis. The monotonous, vicious cycle always repeated itself.

I was on a diet, off my diet, up the scale and down the scale like a yo-yo. And my emotional state fluctuated with the reading on the bathroom scale. On a good day I would feel exhilarated because the scale showed a loss of three pounds. The following day I'd feel a sinking helplessness at the sight of the scale creeping up again. The frustration of not understanding why I couldn't lose the weight and the fear of failing yet another time were the overwhelming emotions I lived with every waking moment of each day.

One of the worst feelings I can remember experiencing was the compulsion to eat when I was already stuffed. I knew this behavior was destructive and totally irrational, but I felt powerless to control my actions.

B*elieving that I obviously lacked*
whatever qualities were
necessary to control myself,
I focused my attention on some future
day when I would have what
it takes to be thin.

The future held the promise of success, but any hope I felt was laced with fear and doubt. I was trapped within a sticky web of time: past failures threatened to repeat themselves, the present became a waiting game, and I was forever impatient for that "someday" when I would finally become the person I wanted to be.

A New Beginning

Then one day I was standing in front of my mirror drying my hair and feeling kind of carefree, when it occurred to me that I had been creating and perpetuating my miserable situation by constantly *dwelling on the problem!* I visualized a scale tipped to one side because of a tremendous imbalance in the weights on either side of it.

The weights on the heavy side symbolized my habitual thoughts about dieting: "Which diet this week? What should I eat today, what should I give up? How long will it take? How many pounds will I lose?" These thoughts were surrounded by a heavy anxiety and fear that I wouldn't be able to lose the weight I wanted to lose, and that I'd never attain the desired image I wanted so badly.

The heavy side of the scale held all the memories of the times I had tried and failed to achieve my goals for weight loss along with the expectation of failing again. The attitude was, "I'm fat, ugly, and stuck here because I don't have the self-control to stop eating. I lack whatever it takes—inner strength, courage, perseverance, patience, energy—but I'm not sure what, and I don't know how to get it." There sat my fat self, fretting and fuming about how hard it is to lose weight while at the same time refusing to give up "fat foods."

On the opposite side of this scale sat my slender self. I envisioned the kind of thoughts and feelings surrounding the image of the person I truly desired to become. She was confident, happy, and satisfied with herself. The slender self longed to emerge victoriously. I could free her by simply refusing to acknowledge the heavy self with all her thoughts, fears, doubts, and discouragement. In other words, I realized that I would become whatever I concentrated on *being*.

If you've ever been on a seesaw with a dubious friend who jumps off without a warning, you can imagine the effect of putting an abrupt end to the "heavy" thoughts by simply saying, "I quit—I'm not playing this game anymore." I realized that if I were to simply let go of the problem—stop thinking and worrying about it—then the solution would appear. If my fat self got off the seesaw, it would suddenly tip to the side where the slender me sat. Then, I could concentrate on *being* this person, instead of wishing I were, because the fat self would simply vanish from the scene, taking all her fat feelings with her.

What happened that day is simply this: I had reached the point where I was sick and tired of thinking about diets, food, what I could and could not eat that day or week, what I should or should not do for exercise, for dinner, for lunch. I simply decided that I would no longer focus my attention on the problem because it was frustrating, boring and a ridiculous waste of my time and energy.

It was the emotion of anger that propelled and inspired me to let go, anger that was no longer directed at myself, but at the stupidity of playing a game I could never win. Now that I had quit, I could see that there were better things to think about and more important things to do with my life.

I decided to change my hairstyle and stop hiding behind "fat clothes." I gave away my old clothes (including the ones I was hoping to fit into "someday") and bought myself new clothes which made me feel prettier and happier. Gradually, as my self-image began to improve, my eating habits improved along with it. My mind was no longer burdened with the aggravation and frustration of my problem. And my emotions were no longer triggered by thoughts of failure and guilt for going off my diet, because I wasn't on one.

I began to focus my attention on other matters—constructive activities such as putting my new-found energy into my career, my family and my friends. Before long, the weight was melting off of me and I was hearing compliments from everyone. My jeans were getting baggy and I had to wear a belt to keep them from falling down. But I didn't mind at all—I loved it! This was the feeling of success I had wanted for so long.

I didn't know it at the time, but I had inadvertently put into practice a principle of power that I now understand quite well. Only later did it occur to me that freeing myself from the endless, self-abusive dialogue and self-criticism for being overweight had other positive effects.

What I had actually begun was a process of **accepting** and **forgiving** myself, of learning to like myself just the way I was right there and then—cellulite, several stomach rolls and all. By turning my attention to other things, I had moved my mind and emotions away from my fat problem, toward the person I wanted to become.

Whatever you habitually think about yourself and your body will affect the way you look, the way you feel, and cause you to behave the way you do. Ultimately, the sum of your actions creates the results you experience. If you're unhappy with those results, it should be obvious that whatever you are thinking, feeling and doing must somehow change before you can experience the results you do want.

Once again, you must use your imagination and emotions to intensify your desire and determination to get out of your rut.

*W hat you really need to lose is a lot
of <u>negative thoughts</u> and
anxious feelings—not just excess
weight. What you need to gain
is greater joy, inner peace and a sense
of knowing that everything is going
to come out okay. You're finally
going to have it your way.*

Take a few moments right now to consider your answers to the following questions. Then jot down your thoughts and answers to these questions in your journal.

1. How do you feel about yourself?

2. How do you feel about your body?

3. When you look in the mirror are you pleased or mildly disgusted with what you see?

4. What do you tell yourself every day about your physical appearance?

5. What do others tell you about the way you look?

6. What do others tell you about who you are as a person?

7. Are you in the habit of scrutinizing your body and criticizing your physical appearance for falling short of some ideal?

8. Do you attempt to conceal every imagined flaw or long to change the way you look?

9. Are you hiding behind "fat clothes" that make you feel ugly and undesirable?

10. Do you constantly discuss your weight problem with friends or family?

If you answered "yes" to questions 7—10 above, take a few more moments to consider why you behave this way. For instance, if you constantly discuss your weight problem with friends and family, is it because you lack other things to talk about? Or is it simply because you have formed the habit of doing so?

Do you think others expect you to feel badly about your situation (and you don't want to disappoint them?) Or do you hope to receive empathy and understanding?

What kind of beliefs about yourself and your body would motivate you to act this way?

Chapter 6

Your Attitude, Actions and Expectations

Now let's explore some of the typical actions you have taken to reach your destination. These actions have been prompted by the type of thoughts and feelings you have written about in your journal.

Can you see where these thoughts and feelings have led you? How has your inner dialogue caused you to behave?

To begin with, you have probably spent a great deal of time defining and labeling the various negative aspects of your problem. You may have labeled yourself as "fat," "grotesque," "out of control," "thirty pounds overweight," "hopelessly addicted to chocolate . . .." Perhaps you have singled out and neatly catagorized certain characteristics of your personality and physical appearance.

Yet, once you form the habit of repeating these labels to define your situation, they only serve to focus your attention and imagination on the undesirable elements of your condition.

L*abels enable you to form images
in your mind that cause
you to identify more and more
with the negative qualities you
want to be free of.*

Your mind will always look for more ways to support these ideas with excuses or explanations for why you are fat, disgusting, out of control. "Well, I inherited the tendency to be obese." "My husband (wife, roommate, mother, father) causes me to eat too much." "I don't get enough exercise." "I have an addictive personality . . .."

Statements like these support the mistaken assumption that you are unworthy or lack some quality you need in order to overcome your problem. Often, they explain your repeated attempts and failures to change your condition by placing the blame on some one or some thing else. Actually, they are merely convenient excuses for failing to take control of your power and direct it wisely.

Where does this type of thinking lead you?

U*nless you take full responsibility*
for your thoughts, feelings,
and actions, you will falsely believe
that you have no control
over yourself or your situation.
You will feel, and seemingly
become, powerlesss.

When you blame your bad habits on outer circumstances or inherent physiological flaws, you have already admitted defeat! Instead of feeling that your desire for
a more slender body is built upon a solid foundation, you
will feel as if you are standing knee-deep in quicksand.
Instead of trusting that everything you need to attain your
desire is already within you, you will feel as if you are
continually sinking and struggling just to survive—and you
will be. Of course, when you're standing in quicksand, the
more you struggle to do anything, the faster you sink.

To achieve and maintain your ideal weight, stop
focusing on the undesirable attributes of your body, yourself
and your situation. You must make the decision to stop
calling yourself names and begin to recognize any comments
you make that define and explain your problem as if you
have no ability or power to overcome it.

Once you refuse to give your power away to food, fat,
fear or outer circumstances and decide to stop making excuses, you will notice the many ways in which you *do* have
control of your mind and emotions. You may even discover

dozens of new ways to direct your misplaced energy toward constructive activity. And never again will you give another thought to food or fat as *your* problem.

Taking a Well-Traveled Road . . ."Going on a diet"

If you have defined your problem as the need to "lose weight," you will look for ways to do just that. Surely you must restrain yourself, give up your favorite foods, or sweat your fat off with exercise (unless you intend to surgically remove it). These actions, however noble, are actually aimed at the symptom (excess fat) instead of the cause of your problem (faulty beliefs about yourself and your body).

You may begin with good enough intentions and decide to go on a diet or follow a diet and exercise regimen for a period of time. And this is precisely the major drawback of going on a diet: it is never your desire or intent to stay on it forever.

Dieting is only a temporary solution aimed at relieving you of the fat without bothering to determine what causes you to overeat to begin with. It takes you on a shortcut which leads right back where you started from—with the same thoughts, feelings and beliefs that cause you to eat more food than your body needs. Sooner or later you have to go *off* a diet since invariably it is an unnatural means of relating to food and living your life as you'd like to.

It is unnatural to have to analyze, criticize, or in some way morally judge every morsel you ingest. The more you have to *think* about food (focus your attention upon it), the less you can allow it to resume its natural importance in your life. You must eat in order to live, and when you are living in order to eat or to keep yourself from eating, something has gone wrong with your thinking.

It is impossible to succeed in losing weight on a diet unless you **desire** and **decide** that dieting is what you want to do, and rarely will you truly desire to be on a diet. As soon as you begin to feel anxious and upset about having to control what you eat, when you eat, how much you eat, or where you eat, you are hardly apt to make a success of your endeavors. The inner conflict and negative emotions you feel are the first clue that you are misdirecting your energy and going against your own inner nature.

To impose an arbitrary restriction on the kind of food you eat (especially a total denial of a particular food that you enjoy) is to invite inner conflict that inevitably leads to failure and frustration. What happens every time you tell yourself, "I can't," "I won't," "I shouldn't" eat this or that? Another part of your mind is asking, "Why not?" and feeling very thwarted.

U*nless you address this inner voice*
and align it with your desire
and decision to be slender,
sooner or later it will sabotage
your success.

A part of being human is to want more, not less, of those things we enjoy. It goes against our nature to feel that we have to give up anything—particularly something we enjoy. The feeling of self-denial and sacrifice leads to inner conflict, and the need to exercise constant self-control leads to confusion. How much of this particular food is okay to eat and how often? What is not okay to eat? Why not? Will I ever be able to enjoy my favorite dessert again?

To further complicate the matter, whatever we try to resist or deny we merely attract and find more difficult to avoid. That's because in order to continually resist it we must think about it! Food can gain a lot of power over us—power that we give it by the sheer fact that we dwell upon it constantly. Remember, "Whatever you try to resist in your mind will persist!"

Whether your desire is to eat certain foods or avoid them, eventually you must learn to put all food in its natural place.

> N*aturally, food belongs in your*
> *stomach when your body is*
> *physically hungry—not when*
> *you are mentally confused,*
> *emotionally distraught or*
> *spiritually starved.*

Expecting Fast Results

Are you in the habit of expecting fast results? Of course, you're anxious to arrive at your destination and want the fastest, easiest, least painful way to lose the excess weight. But starting your journey with this kind of "hurry-up" attitude gets you into trouble before you get started. That's because it conveniently avoids the mental and emotional effort that must be expended in order to pull yourself out of a rut.

With a hurry-up attitude you may look for ways to cut corners and fail to realize that what appears to be the shortest route may actually take you longer or completely fail to get you there. This type of attitude and expectation directs your attention to a feeling of much time and distance between where you are and where you want to be.

Often, the hurry-up approach sets you up for failure because it places demands upon yourself and your body which are unreasonable or entirely unobtainable. Do you constantly remind yourself that you want to lose X number of pounds within X number of days? The pressure to perform within a given time period (usually much too short) often generates a lot of anxiety. And sooner or later this anxiety works against you; it is a form of doubt, fear, and mis-trust which is one of your worst enemies for accomplishing your objectives.

If you truly want answers that will solve your problem for good, you must begin to ask different questions. Instead of asking, "What's the shortest route requiring the least amount of time and effort?" ask, "What faulty beliefs, attitudes and expectations cause me to behave the way I do?"

Confusion Over Various Options and Opinions

Another mistake you can make is to read the opinions of others, follow their advice, and expect a diet or exercise program that works for them to work for you, too. Of course, you wouldn't expect to fit a square peg in a round hole, so why expect to fit yourself or your body into someone else's formula for success?

It isn't realistic to expect to succeed by using any single, rigid formula for weight loss. You use the energy of your mind, emotions and body in a unique combination that can never be precisely duplicated again. And too, unless someone else's idea inspires or rings true to your own inner needs and desires, it is difficult, if not impossible, to make it work for you.

An idea must strike a resonant chord in your mind and emotions before you can use it and make it our own. Therefore, you must design your own unique formula for becoming the person you want to be.

There are countless ways of performing any task you set out to do, but when it comes to making decisions that affect yourself and your body, you must act as your own best authority.

Since you are the one who must live by the choices you make, you should be the final judge of what is right for you.

Who knows more about yourself and your situation than you do? Only you can understand how to fully maximize your inherent strengths and capitalize on your weaknesses. Of course, you can adapt or expand upon the ideas of others, follow general guidelines and learn from their successes or failures, but ultimately you must seek and find your own way of achieving your desires.

Remember the old adage "Believe half of what you see and none of what you hear?" Perhaps it's time to ask yourself why you so often trust the advice or opinions of others more than your own. Is it because these opinions are doled out by so-called "experts?"

Lots of experts in human behavior, psychology and biology have been wrong before, and they will be wrong again. Often they are wrong because when it comes to understanding human behavior they are making an educated guess and documenting their opinions in the name of "scientific" studies. A study may appear to be conclusive evidence of a phenomenon, when actually those who conduct the study have merely sought and found ideas which support their original opinion or hypothesis.

One study published in a national magazine reported that a link had been discovered between obesity and heredity. If you take this study seriously and adopt the belief that heredity is responsible for your overweight condition, you might assume that you are doomed to be overweight forever just because your parents or grandparents are overweight.

What can this type of belief do for you? It can cause you to give up hope, to fail to take responsibility for your actions, and render you "seemingly" powerless to create a positive change in your appearance. Years ago, I would have read this article and accepted the information as fact without questioning whether it was truth or opinion, but not any more.

Every day we are bombarded with so much information that we often feel overwhelmed and confused. Volumes have been written about the subject of weight loss causing us to wonder, "What should I do to get rid of excess fat? Why is it so difficult to maintain my ideal weight?" Not knowing truth from fiction, you may question whether you are doing the "right" thing. You may wonder whether heredity, certain types of food, lack of exercise, lack of willpower, emotional problems, or some combination of these are responsible for your body's condition. Every one of these variables can affect the condition of your body, but when you feel confused about what to do, you may try to do too much or do nothing at all.

Perhaps you have accepted lots of ideas about what you should or should not do, can and cannot do, who or what is to blame for your overweight condition. Once you have tried a number of diets—hoping to succeed, only to fail—you also begin to form your own conclusions about yourself, your body, and weight-loss in general. Yet you must realize that some of the conclusions you have reached may be fact, while others are strictly opinion; some may be true, while others are entirely false ideas about the nature of yourself and your body.

B*eware of any idea that implies a basic limitation or a hopeless situation. Make a conscious effort to identify and discard old worn-out beliefs which assume that you are "lacking" in worth or "limited" in your power to make a permanent change.*

As you do, you will begin to discover the true means of arriving at your destination and staying there.

Now take the next few moments to respond to the following questions. Record your answers in your notebook or journal.

1. How much weight would you like to lose?

2. How much time have you given yourself to do it?

3. What kind of actions have you taken so far? (diet, exercise program, hypnosis, behavior therapy...)

4. Have you succeeded in losing weight with any of these methods?

5. Why do you think this particular method was successful or unsuccessful?

6. What do you think is the cause of your overweight condition? (heredity, bad eating habits, lack of exercise, lack of self-discipline, social circumstances or home environment, emotional problems...)

7. Are there any foods you consider forbidden because they are "fattening"? If so, what are they?

8. Do you attempt to resist these foods even though you really enjoy them?

9. When you read articles or books about dieting, nutrition, mental attitude or exercise, do you feel confused or overwhelmed about what you must do to achieve or maintain your ideal weight?

10. What do *you* believe you should and shouldn't do in order to lose your excess weight forever?

Part IV

Knowing WhereYou Want to Go . . . and Understanding Why

Once we start weaving the gods will furnish the skein.

--Claude Bristol

Chapter 7

The Real Reasons for Losing Weight

Sometimes it's easy to lose sight of the real reasons why you want to lose weight. And if you aren't keeping these reasons in mind, you are bound to lack enthusiasm and the motivation to do it.

Losing weight is not a reward in itself. It's what you believe losing weight is going to give you or do for you that can generate

enthusiasm and provide the motivation to do it.

I believed that by losing weight I would gain self-respect, enjoy a more satisfying social life, boost my career because of increased self-confidence, appear more attractive to myself and others, and be a whole lot happier in general. Yet in the process of trying to lose weight, instead of imagining myself attaining and enjoying these true rewards of being slender, I would visualize my ideal weight on the bathroom scale.

Because I didn't believe I could have what I wanted until I lost the excess weight, I focused my attention on creating a result (losing weight) that had no inherent value to me. In other words, I constantly thought about ways to rid myself of X number of pounds, instead of thinking of ways to gain more confidence, self-respect, and the inner joy I wanted to experience.

What I really wanted more than anything was to be free of the burden of my problem; free of trying to resist my favorite foods, free of feeling fat and guilty, free of being on a diet. What I truly desired was to be able to eat what I like to eat without worrying about the consequences, and (at the same time) look and feel a lot thinner.

What you need to ask yourself is this: How will losing weight add to your life? Once you become who you want to be and your body reflects this inner change, what do you expect to enjoy? Do you hope to experience increased energy, more confidence, the acceptance of others, the joy of enhancing your physical appearance?

Take a moment to think about this. Is it merely weight you want to lose, or is it self-respect you need to gain? Is wearing a size 9, 11, or 14 really meaningful to you? Or is it more important to feel good about who you are and how you look, no matter what size you wear?

Finding Out What You Want and Need

What you want is not simply the experience of weighing X number of pounds. What you want has more to do with satisfying some basic human needs for love, recognition and attention. It comes closer to filling the need to give your own unique talents and abilities a constructive outlet for action. It is actually a longing to use your energy to develop your inner potential to the fullest extent possible—not to store it as fat for future use.

What most of us need to experience is a greater sense of our own inner power and self-worth. We need to feel that we belong in this world and have a purpose for living. We want to know we have the freedom and power to direct our life toward the fulfillment of that purpose. We need love and affection, attention and laughter. We want more energy, more life—not less.

The fulfillment we search for, however, will never be found in food or anywhere "out there" outside of ourselves. But it can be found when the will, mind, emotions and body are working together in harmony and agreement instead of discord and dis-ease. Self-fulfillment can be found inside each one of us, in the **acceptance, forgiveness,** and genuine **love** of the self.

Using Your Imagination the Right Way

If you are measuring your success by some arbitrary number on a scale or weight chart, you are attempting to create something that is merely a suggestion of the real things you desire to have and to be. The creative power of your imagination and emotions can't generate enough desire and enthusiasm for such a vague and meaningless goal as a drop in your weight on the bathroom scale. What will generate sufficient desire and enthusiasm to sustain your motivation to achieve your ideal weight? What exciting changes within your self-image will ultimately affect the shape of your body and bring you the rewards you seek?

Telling yourself you want to weigh X number of pounds is like saying, "I want to be rich." But what exactly is rich? To people who are starving in many nations of the world, everyone in the United States might appear to be rich. Wealth is a relative thing and so is physical weight.

How rich is a net worth of $100,000? It depends on where you live and how you like to live. How thin is 125 pounds? It depends on whether your height is 5 feet or 5 feet, 11 inches. It also depends on whether you live in a culture that considers a slender body lovelier to look at than a pleasantly plump or fat one.

Individuals with anorexia may believe they are fat even when everyone else would agree they are thin. Wealthy individuals can also feel very poor even though by most standards they are quite rich. Again, that's because being thin or rich is first and foremost a state of mind. And there is nothing that can stop you from experiencing that inner state of thought and feeling in your imagination right now, instead of "someday."

*In order to live your dreams and not
just wish for them, you need a
steady source of enthusiasm and
motivation that moves you.
And to generate enthusiasm and
motivation, you must use your
imagination to focus on the joyful
experience of arriving at
your destination and enjoying the
true rewards.*

This means adding a few things to the picture you form in your mind besides a number on the bathroom scale.

Think again about the type of thoughts and feelings that motivate you to plan a vacation you want or need so badly. Notice how your mind begins to focus on the pleasurable feelings of being there, upon the inherent rewards of travel and relaxation. Yet what is inherently pleasurable about weighing X number of pounds or (worse yet) losing X number of pounds? Again, these words are symbolic of the rewards you seek, but the true benefits are so much more than simply reaching a certain physical weight.

Where you want to go is a physical place with a mental and emotional climate. Why you want to go is related to your need to experience a state of mind and emotions that is free of anxiety, fear and frustration. What you want to feel is "at home" in your body and safe within your world. It is a fuller sense of joy and satisfaction that comes from giving yourself permission to experience the love, self-respect and approval that might be missing from your life.

> U*nderstand what truly motivates*
> *you to become the person you*
> *want to be and to have the body*
> *you want to have.*

Breathe some life into your desire with the power of your imagination. Give your desire meaning by believing in the value of its existence. Then back it up with the emotion of confident expectation.

The more clear you can become about what you want and why you want it, the more you will gain a sense of the emotional rewards of having it. The more you can sense these rewards, the easier it will be to generate enthusiasm, faith and the motivation you need to act upon your desire. You will then discover how effortless it can be to achieve it.

What do you believe losing weight (that is, being the person you want to be and having a body to match) will allow you to experience? Take some time to think about this! Yes, you may want to lose weight, but more importantly, you need and want to enjoy the benefits you believe having a slender body will bring you.

The Physical Level of Desire

On a physical level our desire is to experience vibrant health and a sense of well-being. We want to have the physical energy to do the things we enjoy doing, whether it is taking a walk or skiing down a mountain slope. In order to do the things we truly enjoy, we need an abundance of energy, more than what is needed to maintain our daily existence. We want our clothes to fit comfortably without binding or constricting our movement. And we want our outer appearance to reflect the true inner qualities of our own unique personality.

The Emotional Level of Desire

On an emotional level, our desire is to be free of constant frustration, fear and anxiety. What we are really saying and feeling when we are unhappy with our weight is that we want to feel good about who we are. We want to experience the emotional gratification of being at ease with our own physical form.

What matters to our emotional well-being is that we arrive at a point in our perception of our self that feels good, feels secure and comfortable. It is an inner feeling of being in harmony with our own ideal image of our self and our body.

The Mental Level of Desire

On the mental level, our desire is to be free of the burden of dealing with diets and the heaviness of a weight problem. The mind quickly becomes bored by dwelling upon the same old thoughts. It wants to be challenged with new ideas; it wants to be enlightened. The voices within our mind seek agreement and a resolution to inner conflict and confusion.

The mind echoes the longing of our spirit to expand. It naturally desires to know more and to be more, to use its talents and abilities to the fullest and to continue to develop new ones.

The Spiritual Level of Desire

On a spiritual level, our desire is to know our self more completely, to rejoice in being and creating, and to learn how to direct and use our energy constructively.

A natural attribute of all living things is to seek greater fulfillment of life. Behind each of our actions, there is always the desire to experience something more out of life— more love, more money, more happiness, more recognition, more attention, and so on. This desire is often referred to as self-realization or self-actualization; it is the unfolding and outer fulfillment of inner potential.

Our inner spirit desires to be all that it can possibly be. It longs to be nourished, to expand its awareness through the fulfillment of our dreams, to soar like an eagle and claim the glory it deserves. It wants to experience life to the fullest extent and naturally desires spontaneity, joy and freedom.

You must learn to recognize the spiritual essence of your desire. Your inner spirit seeks a state of being that will give you a feeling of love and self-acceptance, relieve you of false guilt and frustration, and win the praise, acceptance and approval of yourself and others. All the beauty that exists within you will attempt to express itself in outer form— through your actions and your physical body.

You can hinder the expression of your inner self if you fail to understand what generates your desire to begin with. Yet when you realize that your desire to be slender is truly the desire of your inner spirit—reflected in every living creature on earth—you will know that achieving it has nothing to do with deserving it. It just *is*. And because you cannot separate yourself from nature, you naturally seek to be more, to have more, and to do more with your life.

Summary of the Real Reasons for Losing Weight

Physical Level of Desire

The need to have physical energy with which to experience life to the fullest. To have the energy to do the things we have always wanted to do. Physical vitality, good health, and a feeling of comfort in our clothing are necessary for our physical well-being.

Emotional Level of Desire

The need to feel inner peace instead of inner conflict. To feel good about who we are. To feel happiness and joy instead of constant frustration, fear, and anxiety. Important to our emotional well-being are the feelings of self-confidence, security, and a sense of belonging in our world.

Mental Level of Desire

The need to learn, to experience joy and a variety of life's pleasures. To be free of the burden of dealing with diets and deprivation. To seek new experiences and expanded awareness.

Spiritual Level of Desire

Fulfillment of the inherent desire of our inner spirit to become all that we are capable of becoming. To experience life to the fullest extent possible by expressing and developing our inner potential.

Chapter 8

Clarify Your Desire: Where Do You Want to Go?

When you venture upon a journey across land or sea, it's rather obvious that you must know where you want to go before you can get there. Yet this is equally as true of the inner journey you are taking.

You must know where you want to go (who you want to be and what you want to experience) before you can get there (think, feel, and act like that person).

Again, you must understand the real reasons why you want to lose weight. Maybe you need to experience a heightened state of self-awareness or self-love. Perhaps you want the acceptance, love and respect of others, a feeling of inner peace and joy, better health, greater self-confidence, or all of the above.

Imagine the physical shape you want to be in. Form a mental image in your mind—a sort of "sensory package" which includes the sight, sound, feel and touch of what you want. Then spend at least five minutes every day focusing on this image. Notice how you feel emotionally as you create these pleasurable thoughts and picture-images within your mind. Doesn't it feel wonderful to imagine having truly achieved your ideal weight?

During this time, you might pretend you are an actor or an actress and act *as if* you are the person you have always wanted to become. Have fun playing the part and feeling what it's like to experience every element of your desire. Try it right now! For the next five minutes, put the power of your imagination to its most practical use.

Clarify your desire to be, to have or to do on every level of your ability to act—mentally, emotionally and physically. Then decide what actions you will take on each level to accomplish your desire.

Your Thoughts

Imagine the kind of thoughts that will occupy your mind once you have lost the weight you want to lose and have become the person you want to be. When your mind is no longer occupied by the need to control your eating habits, what will you constantly think about then? What is your ideal image of your personality, the inner qualities you want to increase and develop? What type of thoughts will replace those you currently think about yourself, about others, or about life in general?

Your Feelings

Consider what it will feel like to have finally achieved your ideal weight. Imagine how you will feel toward yourself and your body. When you are no longer angry and frustrated with the shape your body is in, what type of feelings will you experience then? How will you feel about yourself as a person, about others, and about life in general? Try to experience the typical emotions you will feel every hour of the day, day after day.

Your Body

What will your ideal body look like? How will it feel? Visualize your entire body in the most ideal form that you know it is capable of achieving. Imagine what it's like to live within this ideal body image. Step in to this body; wear it for at least a moment, as often as you can each day. Experience what it will be like to have the kind of body you want to have and the amount of physical energy you want to feel.

In your imagination wear the type of clothing you've been wanting to wear. See yourself expressing your own unique style and personality through your clothes, your posture, your physical presence and poise.

Your Actions

How will your ideal self behave around food? What will you talk about with your family and friends? What will you do with your time and energy? Are you active in sports; do you belong to a gym or attend an aerobics class? How will you react to stress, loneliness, sadness, anger, frustration or despair? Do you express these feelings verbally or find other constructive outlets for expression?

Are you having trouble imagining who you will be or how you will look and act? If so, perhaps you don't believe that you deserve to achieve your desire. Or maybe you feel blocked by a myriad of obstacles that seem to stand in your way.

If you have experienced your ideal weight before, but haven't been there in a long while, perhaps you have forgotten how it feels. If you've never been happy with the body you have, perhaps you doubt that you ever will be. Identify these obstacles and decide to face them once and for all!

Keep trying to clarify a visual and sensual image of your desire. Persist until you get in touch with the feelings, sensations and true rewards of being there. With practice it does get easier. So try and try again as if your health and happiness depend on it. Because they do depend on you—on your willingness to have in your imagination what you want in your reality.

If you can imagine yourself lying on a warm sandy beach, you can imagine yourself experiencing the joy of having the physical form you want and a personality to go with it. Forming a clear mental, emotional, and physical image enables you to:

1. Focus upon your objectives instead of the obstacles in your way, thus increasing your power to achieve them with the energy of your attention and focus of concentration.

2. Generate and sustain the enthusiasm and motivation you need to persist until you achieve your desire. The emotional elements of anticipation and expectation inspire you to take action upon your desire.

3. Recognize and perceive the potential of your desire within yourself so that you are ready and willing to receive and accept it as your reality.

In so many words, making a clear decision about your destination makes it easier to get there, and also let's you know when you've arrived.

Arriving at Your Destination

Instead of fretting about the need to lose weight, you can start becoming the person you want to be right now. But first you must know who you want to be and realize that you *can* be that person. The power to develop and express your finest qualities is within you now or you wouldn't have the desire in the first place. It merely awaits your recognition, attention and conscious direction.

D*on't make the mistake of believing*
you need to lose weight before you
can experience happiness, inner peace
and self-acceptance. This faulty belief
will keep you enslaved to endless
misery and frustration.

The truth is that you need to experience a feeling of inner joy, peace and self-acceptance before you can lose weight and keep it off for good.

Each time you imagine and feel the benefits of your desire in the present moment you move a step closer to your destination. Since your power to act is in the present moment why wait for that "someday" to come along? In truth, it never will as long as you keep projecting it into the future, far ahead of where you are.

Make a commitment to redirect your energy—your thoughts, feelings, and actions—toward the attainment of your objectives, and food will automatically lose its power and importance in your life.

The power to make yourself feel good really does belong to you. Don't give it away to food, meaningless numbers on a scale or weight chart, outer circumstances, or other people. Own it now. Take back all the energy you put into thinking about food, fat and diets, and put it into living your life as you have always wanted it to be.

Your choice in this moment is to be free of dieting and excess weight forever. That choice will be your experience as you **believe** in it, as you direct your imagination and emotions to own it now—not tomorrow. Live "as if" you are your future self and no obstacle can stand in your way. The dream is already yours.

Choosing the Contents of Your Mind

The contents of your mind is like a rich and fertile field where ideas are sown and blossom with the focus of your attention. Look around the field of your mind. There you will find ideas which lift you up and bring you joy, and others that bring you down and leave you in misery. Notice the difference in their colors, how they make you feel and what they lead you to do.

Has the soil of your mind become so hardened that only weeds can grow there? Break up the soil (your current habits of thought and feeling) and plant new seeds of thought and feeling that will bring you greater joy. Uproot the weeds and make room for more flowers.

Recognize those ideas that empower and inspire you to express your inner potential. Pull out the ones that keep you from feeling joy and the sunlight that surrounds you. It may take effort and courage to uproot old ideas of lack and limitation, but it takes even more to maintain them.

Make time to plant new seeds of thought that will breed success and beauty. Nurture them with your love and imagine them growing within you everyday. Focus your energy and attention on the seeds of thought that match your life as you choose to live it. And with faith and perseverance, the seeds that you love and nurture will inevitably come into your life in full bloom.

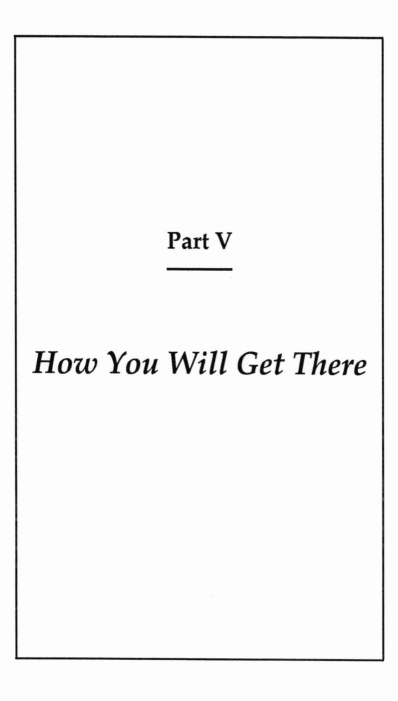

Part V

How You Will Get There

The subconscious mind embodies the feeling and wisdom of the past, the awareness and knowledge of the present and the thought and vision of the future.

--Claude Bristol

Amber-Allen Publishing
P.O. Box 6657
San Rafael, California 94903-0657

We hope that you have enjoyed this book. If you would like to order a copy for a friend or be informed about other publications from Amber-Allen, simply fill in and mail this card today.

☐ Please send me _____ copy(ies) of **Free of Dieting Forever** @ $9.95 each plus $2.00 shipping and handling. (California residents please add 6% sales tax.)

☐ Please keep me informed about other publications from Amber-Allen.

Name _____

Address _____

City _____ State _____ Zipcode _____

Enclosed is my check in the amount of $ _____ made payable to Amber-Allen.
Please allow six weeks for delivery.

Chapter 9

Acknowledge the True Problem

The first step in solving a problem is to acknowledge it. From there you can determine your objectives, decide to do something about it, and then do it.

Consider for a moment whether you have honestly acknowledged your problem. All too often we develop a mind-set when it comes to dealing with our problems. (The dictionary defines a mind-set as "a fixed mental attitude formed by experience, education, or prejudice.") Our habits of perception can block out information and ideas that may play a key role in arriving at a solution.

Again, if you define your problem as the need to lose weight, you may say, "I'm much too fat, I've got to get rid of

this excess weight. I need to lose 20 pounds." Sound familiar?
Yet the habit of perceiving your problem as the need to lose
weight leads to the habit of seeking certain types of solutions.
Going on a diet, giving up your favorite foods or getting rid
of the fat are the typical solutions to a problem defined as the
need to lose weight. The focus is always on the food or the
fat: giving up certain foods or getting rid of excess fat become
the main objectives.

Excess fat is treated as if it's a disease-like condition
that must be removed as quickly as possible. Food is
regarded as good, bad, fattening or non-fattening and
credited with much more power than it could possibly have.

> F*ood and fat become the culprits that*
> *must be avoided, attacked or*
> *placed under control, while little or*
> *no attention is given to the*
> *state of your mind and emotions.*

Remember, the motivating force behind your desire
to lose weight must come from the rewards you expect to
experience. If what you truly desire is a sense of personal
fulfillment, increased confidence and self-respect, and a
physical form that feels comfortable, agile, and attractive to
you, then why define your problem as the need to lose
weight? Why not state your purpose as the desire to achieve
these things instead?

This gives you a clear mental image of what it is you
are truly after, and turns your "problem" into an opportunity
to accomplish wonderful things. "I want to gain a greater

sense of purpose and direction in my life; I want to increase the amount of love and respect I have for myself and my body; I want to have a healthier, more beautiful body."

When you state your intention as a positive action that can be taken, it's easier for your mind to visualize and attain the results you want. After all, doesn't it sound more rewarding to focus on what you can have than to think about what you must lose? Isn't it easier to believe you can do something, than to believe you can undo something? Isn't it more enjoyable to direct your imagination toward images of what you do want instead of what you don't?

Stating your **desire** in terms of a positive result you intend to enjoy instead of a negative result you need to overcome changes your attitude and feelings about the goal and gives you a clear image of the objective you want to attain. This sets your mind to look for these things until you actually find them within you.

It's far easier to generate enthusiasm for creating an image of a slender, healthy body and the true rewards you seek than it is to be enthusiastic about losing weight, going on a diet, weighing 125 pounds, or losing 30 pounds.

To our mind and emotions, the action of losing weight can be difficult to picture and *feel* taking place in our imagination. Again, the words "losing weight" are symbolic of the true rewards of being a certain person and having a certain kind of body, but they fall short when it comes to providing the mental and emotional energy necessary to do this.

Ask yourself what it feels like to lose weight. Then ask yourself what it feels like to be happy instead of miserable, to feel comfortable in your clothing, to be complimented by others, to be free of the burden of inner conflict, to feel confident in the company of others, and you may catch a glimpse of what it feels like to be the person you want to be.

Imagine what it's like to sit at a table full of your favorite foods and eat only what you need to satisfy your physical hunger. As you visualize yourself as the person you want to become, you begin to activate the change within you even though its outer reflection will take some time to appear.

Remember the last time you needed a haircut? If not, pretend that you need one right now. Do you find yourself visualizing the way your hair will look after it's cut—or do you think of the action of cutting your hair and removing so many inches of growth? Usually your mind will wander automatically toward images of the result you want, how you want to look and feel afterward. If all you could think of is cutting (losing or getting rid of) excess hair, why would you bother to do it at all? There must be the reward of a better appearance or the experience of having your hair feel a certain way against your face and body.

Focusing your attention on such a vague and meaningless desire as losing weight fails to give you the incentive to do it. More than that, it keeps you locked into a mind-set of seeking the same solutions and conveniently avoids the true problem. You become caught in a vicious circle that takes you nowhere and gives you nothing for your effort but more grief.

There is no relief except to acknowledge the truth, and make a decision to jump out of this pattern of thinking once and for all. It's time to break the habit of defining your problem as the need to lose weight and discard it for a better way.

Something has been missing from the way you habitually describe your problem. And that hidden variable is absolutely necessary for arriving at a solution.

Redefining The Problem

Start with an open mind. Set all of your opinions (and those of others) aside for now. Forget about all your failures and start with a clean slate. **Forgive** yourself for attempting to create a permanent change in the shape of your body with the limited, short-sighted vision you have focused on so far. It's finally time to identify and acknowledge the true issues that must be addressed.

The true problem is not that you weigh too much, and it's not that you need to lose weight.

> The true problem is that you
> unwittingly and habitually
> create and perpetuate your
> overweight condition with
> a set of faulty beliefs about yourself
> and your body.

These faulty beliefs fill your mind with images of deficiency and feelings of doubt and fear. They keep your attention and concentration on the obstacles in your way instead of the power you have to become the person you want to be and to have the body you want. Faulty beliefs cause you to direct your power (your thoughts, feelings, expectations and actions) in reverse—leading you away from your destination and toward your fears.

Listed below are some of the many ways to more accurately describe and define the problem. Each is related to the true problem and is meant to help you identify and acknowledge it with more clarity and accuracy than merely the need to lose weight. Each is an aspect of misdirecting your power or misunderstanding how it operates to create what you want.

There are many ways of saying the same thing, but often only one of these will strike you as a truth you can relate to. The problem will first be defined by what it is and then by what it isn't. The key is to find a way to view your situation from a new perspective, a heightened awareness that can easily lift you up and carry you away from it for good.

The Problem Is . . .

You may be clinging to a set of faulty beliefs and they cling to you, attracting more ideas of a similar nature. You may believe in false ideas about yourself, your body, and food and weight loss in general. These self-limiting, self-critical and self-defeating beliefs are at the root of all your problems. They sound like this: "I am a failure, I lack something, I can't do it, I don't deserve."

Faulty beliefs create and perpetuate a poor self-image and a lack of self-esteem. A poor self-image can lead to a lack of self-approval and acceptance, self-confidence, self-trust and genuine self-love.

Perhaps you believe you can achieve your ideal weight, but fail to back it up with action. Or you take plenty of action such as dieting and exercise, with your feelings and faith opposed to your action (that is, filled with anxiety, doubt, and the expectation of failure).

You may constantly dwell upon the problem, increasing and perpetuating it with the energy of your thoughts and feelings. What you concentrate upon is what you get. You are what you think you are because you give energy and power to these thoughts. The good news, however, is this: as you focus on who you want to become, these inner qualities will increase in power and be effortlessly created in your body's image.

You may imagine your body as less than what it could be, dwell upon its less desirable qualities, and thus reinforce and perpetuate them because you focus your attention upon them. This habit of thinking forms an inner image in your mind that is reflected in your actions, and ultimately in the outer image (physical condition) of your body.

You may have the habit of perceiving and defining your problem as if you have no control. This sense of powerlessness affects the type of solutions you accept as logical and leads to the habitual ways you have so far attempted to overcome the problem such as dieting. You may say, "I want to lose weight" and automatically associate "dieting" with that desire. The word "dieting" may carry emotional overtones and negative connotations associated with previous experience that can set you up for failure before you begin.

You may be a sensitive, sensuous and loving person with needs that aren't being met. In your desire to fill the void and empty feeling within, you turn to food when what you really need is more love, more attention, more physical affection (more kisses, hugs, and the warmth of touching). You may eat chocolate when what you truly crave is an outlet for expressing your warm and "sweet" personality.

You may think you are always hungry for food when what you are starving for is more life, more laughter, more love.

You may use your excess weight to shield and insulate you from failure and hurt, disappointment, social interaction or true intimacy. If you live in fear of these things and expect to experience them, fat can become a convenient way to avoid dealing with sensitive issues.

> Y *ou may expect to lose weight without giving yourself what you truly want and need. Food may be acting as a substitute for the fulfillment of a real inner need.*

Find out what the true need is. Satisfy your need for self-love and a sense of purpose, passion, and direction in your life. Once you do, you won't want or need to overeat. You won't use food to slow you down or put the brakes on your energy. Nor will you want to store your energy (in the form of excess fat) for future use.

You may have unrealistic expectations with regard to yourself, your body, dieting, food and weight loss in general. Perhaps you expect your body to gain five pounds by eating a four-ounce candy bar (impossible), or expect it to lose five pounds by doing something to it that is equally unreasonable (like starving it or forcing it to sweat).

You may have failed to lose weight or maintain your ideal weight in the past, and expect to fail again in the future.

You may project past failures into the future when you could and should be expecting success.

You may dwell on the past or live in the future when your only power to take action exists in the present. When you spend too much time in the past or future, inevitably you sink into fear, doubt, frustration and insecurity. You will feel powerless because you can't control your actions when they are way ahead of you (or way behind). There is never any fear when you live in the present moment. Fear simply fades away in the light of today.

You may misdirect your creative energy (your powers of belief, thought, feeling and action), because you are ignorant of your power, you refuse to accept responsibility for it, or you fail to focus, direct and apply it in a constructive manner.

You may be afraid to express your personal power. You may believe that if you expressed your true personality and feelings without holding back, others may be harmed or simply leave you. They may be hurt by your success and happiness or threatened by the strength of your energy. When you change who you are, your relationships with those who are close to you will also change. Perhaps you doubt whether you can handle this change or seriously question whether others can.

You may seek quick and easy solutions to your pain and frustration. And in your haste to save time and energy you end up spending far more than you would ever spend if you would slow down and take the time to redirect the focus and force of your mind and emotions.

You may have little or no faith in the wisdom of your subconscious mind to guide you toward your ideal weight, and maintain it for you without conscious effort.

You may be inadvertently applying your power in reverse and have simply formed the habit of doing so. Once you make a decision to break this habit and direct your energy toward constructive activities, you are on your way to success. It's that simple.

The Problem Isn't ...

It isn't simply that your body is fat; but you may think, believe, feel and act *as if* you are fat... and so you are. Outer experience will always reflect the inner state of your mind and emotions. Your actions will follow your beliefs.

It isn't that you lack self-discipline, perseverance or courage. Nor that you are guilty of some terrible sin, unworthy of success, undeserving of joy, or unlovable. Rather, the problem is that you may think you are. When you believe and have faith in these ideas, you act accordingly and thus receive what little sense of joy and accomplishment you expect to receive.

It isn't that you have failed in the past, but that you expect to experience the same pattern of failure in the present and continue to project it into the future with the extraordinary power of your imagination and emotions. (Your imagination enables you to focus your energy upon your desire; your emotions are the invisible force that draws it to you).

It isn't that you lack the power or potential to overcome your weight problem, but you may fail to recognize that you are endowed with the power to create your own happiness and misery. You may simply misdirect your power—unconsciously and unintentionally.

It isn't that the problem exists outside of you, beyond your control, but you may have the habit of blaming outside circumstances and endlessly searching for answers outside of yourself.

It isn't a question of how to lose weight, but rather how to become the person you want to be—first in your imagination so that it will naturally become your reality.

It isn't a question of how you will become the person you want to be in some vague and distant future, but how to feel and imagine being there right now, in this moment, and then the next, and the next.

Solutions That Will Set You Free Forever

As you read the following section, choose any solution or combination of solutions that feels right to you. This is an important part of the process of clarifying your desire to be, to have and to do. As you define the potential solutions you are willing to accept in your life, you will open up new avenues of direction for action to follow.

You will also want to look for your own ways to define the solution. Choose an action that you want to take, and you will find it easier to generate the enthusiasm and motivation you need to persist until you succeed.

The Solution Is . . .

Become aware of the false and limiting beliefs you entertain about yourself, your body and food and weight loss in general. Be willing to discard these ideas (you might imagine pulling them out by the roots), and replace them with constructive, self-liberating and empowering beliefs.

Love and **accept** your body as is. Begin to think, feel and act as if you are the person you want to become. As you focus your attention on these new ideas and actions, you form and strengthen new habit-patterns that will surely replace the old.

Make a **commitment** to redirect your creative energy (powers of thought, feeling and imagination) in a forward manner, with clear purpose and intent, **faith** and action.

Develop **trust** in the wisdom and power of your subconscious mind to automatically guide you toward your ideal weight through your intuition and impulses toward action.

Stop dwelling upon your problem with food and fat and put your creative energy into constructive activities—new hobbies and outside interests.

Recreate your body's image with the power of your imagination in the shape that you do want instead of the one you don't want. Imagine your body as the best it can be, and then dwell on this inner image in your mind and emotions.

Learn to accept responsibility for your situation and stop blaming other people or outer circumstances for your current situation.

Break up old patterns of behavior (including habits of thought, feeling and action) and direct your attention toward new and exciting endeavors. Once you choose a solution that will work for you and focus your mind on the solution instead of the problem, you will reach your objectives in no time at all.

Discover the needs you have that aren't being met and clarify your desire and decision to fulfill them.

Boost your self-image to new heights by **accepting** yourself as you are right now, by **trusting** your inner self to guide you toward your ideal weight, and by giving your exterior appearance a "new look" (hair style, clothing, make-up).

Forgive yourself and let go of false guilt by realizing that whatever you believe you are guilty of was due to a misunderstanding or misdirection of your creative energy. It was simply a reverse application of the principles of personal power.

Drop your old expectations with regard to yourself, your body, diets, food and weight loss in general.

Decide that you will break the habit of criticizing yourself for falling short of your ideal image.

Form the habit of focusing your attention on becoming all that you can be instead of wishing that you could be someone else.

Forget about how you will lose weight and trust that you will become the person you want to be—not in some vague and distant future—but right now!

Know that you already have whatever it takes to become the person you desire to be. You only need to recognize this potential, and be willing to **accept** it for yourself.

Forget the failures of the past and **expect** to experience tremendous success from this point on.

Recognize that you have the power to create your happiness and your misery according to the manner in which you focus and direct your energy and attention.

Stop discussing your weight problem; stop saying you are fat and out of control—whether you say it to yourself or to others.

Make a decision to replace your current destructive inner dialogue and fearful and frustrated emotional tone with constructive thoughts and feelings that will bring you the results you want.

The Solution is Not . . .

The solution to your weight problem is not to give up anything; it is to have something more; to reveal the answers that exist within you and recognize your power and ability to overcome this problem.

The solution is not to go on a diet, but to ask your inner self (the wisdom of your subconscious mind) to guide you toward your ideal weight.

The solution is not to look for ways to discipline your compulsion to eat, but rather to listen to your body's inner messages of true hunger instead of outer signals that it's time to eat.

> T*he solution is not to judge or criticize yourself for failing to achieve your ideal weight; it is to look for ways to appreciate yourself and your body; to find new ways of fulfilling the emotional needs that aren't being met.*

The solution is not to strive to lose or get rid of weight, but rather to gain and enhance your self-esteem and self-image and thus easily, automatically transform your body's image.

The solution is not a quick remedy to rid yourself of excess fat but is an ongoing, never-ending process of learning how to manage your energy wisely.

Chapter 10

Remove the Obstacles In Your Way

The true obstacles to achieving and maintaining your ideal weight live within your imagination. Every time you imagine an obstacle, recall previous failures, or conjure up images of what you don't want, you bring these images into your mind and emotions, and eventually into your experience. All too often, you can make the innocent mistake of misdirecting your energy away from your desire by dwelling upon what you fear will happen. As you focus upon the fear, you increase its power and move yourself toward it.

Think of your mind, emotions and body as forms of power that you can apply in both forward (constructive) or reverse (non-constructive) directions. Can you see how non-constructive habits of thought and feeling are the true obstacles to your success?

T o remove the obstacles in your
way, you must acknowledge
the power of your imagination and
emotions and make a decision to
direct them constructively.
Unless you recognize the power of
your thoughts and feelings, you will
hardly make an effort to use
that power wisely.

It may seem that external forces beyond your control operate against you or stand in your way of success. Yet your beliefs and expectations are always mirrored in your experience. If you believe, for example, that you are unable to resist the temptation to eat an entire box of chocolate candy (instead of one or two pieces), you will act on that belief by eating an entire box of candy. Your belief is then reinforced by your experience, and it will seem that your original assumption was valid all along.

At first it may be difficult to recognize when your power is operating in reverse, so the following paragraphs will briefly describe some of the common ways this can occur. Keep in mind that these non-constructive habits of thought, feeling, and action can always be stopped, turned around, and put into forward motion.

The True Obstacles to Your Success

Conflicting and Vague Desires

If you have a desire to eat more food than your body needs *and* a desire to be slender, you have conflicting desires. The desire that is backed with the strongest emotion, given more attention, and thus acted upon will be the one you ultimately experience. You must clearly decide between one or the other and use your emotions to support this decision.

Lack of Commitment

There is incredible power in the act of making a firm decision or commitment to your goal. Failure to make a firm commitment may stem from vague or incompatible desires, weak intent, purpose, and lack of motivation. If you will clarify your desire, intent and purpose, you will discover your primary motivation and find it easier to make a commitment to achieve it.

A Sense of Futility

This feeling comes from the false belief that you are powerless. If you truly believed you could be the person you want to be, no doubt you would already be that person. Try to sense the power within you that desires to achieve and maintain a body weight that feels more comfortable to you. That power is real. You can put it into forward motion with a clear desire and firm decision.

Fear and Doubt

There are times when you may want something so badly and yet believe you will never get it. You may hope it will happen, yet experience a lot of fear that you won't have it or doubt that you deserve it. Too much fear and doubt can neutralize your good intentions, and cause you to take actions that bring about your fear instead of your desire. You must learn to relax and free yourself from constant anxiety— the kind that drives you to overeat, as well as the kind that drives you to diet.

Lack of Self-Esteem

You cannot have what you will not accept for yourself. And you will not accept your desire as long as you believe you don't deserve it. The beliefs you have about yourself and your body are backed by strong emotions. It is going to take equally strong emotions to replace non-constructive beliefs with constructive ones. It's going to take self-love to replace self-hate, forgiveness to replace guilt, joy to replace despair, and inspiration to replace frustration. Know that your desire to be more and to have more is compatible with the inherent desire of all living things.

Lack of Faith

You may be so wrapped up in the darkness of your problem that you fail to see the light of a solution that has existed all along. This can come from too much dependency upon the rational, logical mind to bring about your desire. You must learn to develop more faith in your subconscious, inner self.

Living in the Past or the Future

In the realm of your imagination, you have the ability to remember (hindsight) and to look forward (foresight) to events. Within your mind, you can literally re-live the past and dwell in the future, and yet forget that your power to act is in the present. Fear gathers power as you dwell on mistakes of the past or project them to the future. Faith is much easier to maintain when you live in the present.

Conscious Striving and Control

Conscious striving and control is a result of a lack of faith in your inner self to guide you. Because you can't always see the path you must travel or know what steps you must take to attain your desire, you may think you have to strive, struggle and control your actions every inch of the way. Not true!

Force of Habit

We are creatures of habit, and mind-sets are a common affliction. You may spend your days with your power in reverse simply because you are in the habit of doing so. You can break this habit by making a firm decision to release old destructive patterns and embrace new constructive ones. Make a conscious decision to form new habits of thinking, and soon new patterns of behavior will follow.

Projection and Association With Prior Experience

There is a natural tendency to associate a current situation with previous experience and thus project or expect that the same result will occur in the future. In your imagination you may visualize and believe that the future will bring the same events you have experienced in the past. If your past experience has been filled with obstacles, frustration, and failure, it's easy to imagine there is more to come.

Concept of Time and Distance

You may continually project the attainment of your desire into the future because you doubt that you are worthy of it right now. You may falsely believe you have to travel great distances, climb insurmountable obstacles, sacrifice months or years of your life, or "pay your dues" before you can have what you want.

Guilt and Self-Condemnation

Guilt is a form of self-punishment that often lingers long after the "wrongful" deed is done. Rarely does it serve a practical or constructive purpose. Although it may not be easy to forgive yourself for a lifetime of mistakes, it isn't any easier to spend the rest of your life carrying the burden of guilt for making them.

Putting Your Power In Forward Gear

When it comes to achieving and maintaining your ideal weight, there is a way to apply your power in forward gear. You can form new habits of constructive thought that will surely move you toward your desire—efficiently, painlessly, and permanently.

On the following page is a summary of your power in forward and reverse gears. Each phrase describes a particular kind of mental-emotional state, a mood or outlook, an attitude or an expectation.

As you read over the summary, make an effort to experience the feeling behind each word or phrase. Think about the predominant mood and attitude you have experienced today. Then consider some of the ways in which you have used your power in both forward and reverse gears.

These same principles apply to all areas of your life. You can put your power in forward gear to attain whatever desire you may have.

Summary of Your Creative Powers

Constructive Use Of Energy	**Non-Constructive Use Of Energy**
Your Power in Forward Gear	*Your Power in Reverse Gear*

	Constructive Use Of Energy	**Non-Constructive Use Of Energy**
Mental Level of Action	A clear desire and intent to achieve your goal	Conflicting or vague desires; wishes
	Sense of purpose	Sense of futility
	Strong intent and determination	Weak intent and lack of determination
	Imagining the best outcome	Imagining the worst outcome
	Visualization of the ideal	Visualization of the obstacles
	Focus of attention on what you desire and intend to do	Focus of attention on what you cannot do or what you fear will happen
Emotional Level of Action	Decisiveness	Inability to decide what you want
	Commitment to attain your desire	Inability to make a firm commitment
	Faith and acceptance of your desire	Fear and doubt that your desire is coming
	Expectation of success	Expectation of failure
	Love and self-respect	Hate and self-contempt
	Grateful attitude	Ungrateful attitude
	Self-forgiveness and release	Guilt and self-condemnation
	Feeling worthy of happiness and success; healthy self-esteem	Feeling unworthy of happiness and success; denial of self-worth
Physical Level of Action	Self-praise	Self-criticism
	Releasing energy through action	Blocking energy through inaction
	Speaking of desires to self	Speaking of fears to others
	Affirming personal strengths	Affirming personal weaknesses
	Exuberant exercise and activity	Inactivity and lethargy

In reality, these actions are not so neatly separated. Here they have been divided among levels merely to illustrate this point: Your beliefs, thoughts, feelings and actions are powerful forms of energy that constantly shape your body as well as your life. Together they form an overall mood or attitude that pervades your life, determines your behavior, and ultimately creates the results you experience.

Have you been spinning your wheels or spending your time in reverse gear? If so, don't judge yourself as right or wrong or make yourself feel terrible for doing so. Most of us experience all of these attitudes and feelings at one time or another, to one degree or another.

T*he important thing is to recognize*
when you are putting your
power in reverse. Then you can
choose to turn it around and
spend more time in forward gear
than you do in reverse.

You can't stop your mind from thinking, but you can become aware of the quality of your thought and consciously choose what you will think about. You can't stop yourself from feeling, but as you change the quality of your thought your feelings and actions will follow.

For better or worse, your predominant thoughts and feelings will be reflected in your body and your circumstances. You are the only one with the power to make these change for the better.

The Attitude You Have Toward Your Body

Your physical body—how you look, how you feel, the amount of energy you have to accomplish your goals—is critical to your enjoyment of life. It is difficult, if not impossible, to ignore your body and its needs, and yet it is easily taken for granted, that is, until a problem develops which robs you of the health and vitality you're accustomed to. Then suddenly you may realize how important and how precious your body really is.

How often do you stop to consider the awesome beauty of your physical form instead of its lack and limitations? Why don't you perceive your body as a miracle of life and treat it with the love and respect it deserves?

The attitude you have toward your body begins to develop at an early age—before you are mature enough to form your own ideas or comprehend how ridiculous and mistaken the attitudes of others might be. As a child, you begin to accept the beliefs of your parents, peers, and culture without questioning whether these have any truth, merit or substance. Often they do not, and you may learn to regard your body as somehow tainted, distasteful or disgusting.

Quite unconsciously, you begin to accept others' opinions of what constitutes beauty and then constantly judge yourself against this ideal model. You may compare every unique feature you own against the ideal features you consider worthy of admiration. And these opinions are rarely questioned once they are adopted as your own.

The media bombards you with images of the idealized version of beauty; and you watch, filled with shame, if your body appears less than picture-perfect. Where is it written that you must look a certain way in order to be worthy of love, self-dignity and the acceptance of others? Who in this world has the right to dictate what you should or should not look like?

It doesn't matter what others think or say about how you look, but you give them this power over you when you falsely believe their opinion is important. Once the opinions of others become a measure of your self-worth, you experience inner conflict and confusion because it's impossible to live up to anyone else's ideal image.

Instead you must realize that no ideal image in human form exists anymore than does an ideal image of a dog or cat. If you could ask one million owners of different breeds of dogs and cats which one is the most beautiful, intelligent, adorable creature on earth, you would likely get one million different answers.

The only body image you can create is the one you imagine and believe to be ideal for you. You wouldn't expect your mind to be an exact duplicate of some ideal brain. Why should you expect your body to conform to some ideal body image? Each human mind and personality is unique and so is every human body. Consequently, the only thing that you can hope for is to make the most of what you have and be the best that you can be.

Do you seek the acceptance of others as if your life or happiness depends on it? If so, you are wasting your time and energy trying. Your life and happiness depend on nothing of the sort. What they do depend on are self-approval, self-acceptance and self-love.

The opinions of others may be worthless to you, but your own opinions are not. You cannot control what others think of you, but you do control what you think of yourself. Others may or may not appreciate your unique form of beauty, but it doesn't matter as long as you do.

> *What truly matters is what you think of yourself and repeatedly say to yourself every hour of the day, every day of the year, and how you feel when you are saying it.*
> *It matters because these repetitive thoughts and feelings will be reflected in your body's health and appearance.*

At one time fat was fashionable; but since the present infatuation is with being thin, you might falsely believe the measure of your beauty corresponds directly with a low number on the bathroom scale.

Who is truly beautiful anyway? The person who **believes** they are! Ultimately one's inner belief in beauty and self-worth (self-respect, appreciation, recognition of personal power and self-esteem) will radiate as outer beauty. It is this kind of inner quality that others find so attractive.

Perhaps you find it easier to focus on each tiny flaw instead of the larger realization that you inhabit a truly miraculous creation. Of course, the only reason it's easier is because you have already formed the habit of thinking this way. This habit can be broken with the desire, decision and determination to do so. It can be replaced with new habits of thinking.

Fortunately, your body continues to sustain you regardless of your current opinion of it. But as you learn to praise yourself and honor your physical form with the love and gratitude it truly deserves, you will be amazed at how well and how quickly it responds.

Chapter 11

Free Yourself From Guilt

If you truly want to achieve and maintain your ideal weight without dieting, it's time to feel good about who you are and how you look right now. It's time to **accept** yourself as you are, instead of criticizing yourself for falling short of an ideal image given to you by others.

It's time to **forgive** yourself for being out of shape and appreciate the finer qualities you do have. It's time to be free of the guilt you feel . . .

for gaining too much weight to begin with,
for failing to lose weight by dieting,
for refusing to do anything about it sometimes,
for continuing to overeat and under-exercise,
for saying one thing and doing another.

The constant barrage of self-criticism you shout at yourself (audibly or not) is the product of perceived failures you have experienced again and again. But you can decide to break this habit of self-abusive self-criticism once and for all. You can stop blaming yourself for all the times you've tried and failed, because you haven't committed any crimes, and you aren't guilty of anything!

This doesn't mean you aren't responsible for your actions; it only means it isn't necessary to beat yourself up for making innocent mistakes. Your failure to stick to a diet or your decision last week to give up a favorite food doesn't make you guilty of being an overweight, undisciplined, unattractive, poor example of the human race.

Imagine giving your best friend a powerful set of tools with which to perform a task within a certain period of time. If you neglect to show him how to use the tools to accomplish the task quickly and efficiently, would you berate and criticize him for failing to get the job done on time?

If your friend—lacking instruction and oblivious to danger—picks up the tools anyway and carelessly injures himself because he doesn't understand how to use them to safely accomplish the task at hand, would you scream and yell and blame him for his mistakes?

Perhaps you would, but the point is this: you are using a unique and powerful set of tools to create your life, to mold and form the events that shape not only your experience, but the condition of your body. These tools are your mind, emotions and body through which you take action to create results. These tools are the ideas you hold to be true about reality, about yourself and your body, ideas which are self-perpetuating unless you make an effort to discard or replace them.

With or without your conscious awareness, you are using your "power tools" every moment of your life. And you can learn to use them more consciously and more skillfully to create the results you do want.

The Reason Why You Fail

You want to be free of your weight problem. You may believe you can do it and set for yourself the task of losing a certain number of pounds within a given period of time. Perhaps you start out with good intent, sufficient desire, and lots of enthusiasm, but fail again and again to complete the task successfully. Why do you keep failing? Who or what is to blame?

You fail because you have never been given an owner's manual on how to use your tools constructively. You have allowed your imagination and emotions to focus on what you don't want, and therefore fail to take consistent action toward achieving your ideal weight. You fail simply because you haven't learned how to use your power to create the results you do want: a slender body without giving up the foods you love or the emotional gratification you get from eating them.

While you work at accomplishing your goal you think about the weight you want to lose, think about the times you have tried and failed, think about the foods you can and cannot eat. And all the while you feel the frustration, deprivation, and anxious emotions that are contrary to your goal of thinking, feeling and acting like the slender person you want to become.

Perhaps you are oblivious to the beliefs about yourself and your body that are out of alignment with your desire to lose weight. You may need or want this desire, yet believe you don't deserve it or have what it takes to achieve it. You may believe in your ability to achieve your ideal weight, yet doubt your capacity to maintain it.

W*hen you want one thing and*
believe in another, when
you think about succeeding while
believing and expecting
(quite unconsciously at times) that
you are bound to fail again,
you will fail again.

To get the results you want, you have to use your tools in the only way they can work for you, instead of letting them work against you. Your beliefs must be in harmony with your desire. Your particular set of tools—beliefs, thoughts, feelings and expectations must be taken out, honestly assessed and adjusted for alignment with the task. If there wasn't something wrong with the way you have been using them, the job would have been completed long ago.

The Self-Fulfilling Prophecy

It's possible to use your tools so carelessly that you actually do more harm than good. For example, when you blame your failures on inherent flaws or a weak character; when you turn the anger, resentment and frustration you feel inward upon yourself, you deplete your self-confidence and lower your self-esteem.

This type of behavior becomes a "self-fulfilling prophecy." The belief that you are weak, unworthy or lacking something makes it easy to abuse yourself and your body by over-indulging in food. Then as you gain weight (and seemingly lose power to control yourself), you eat more and more!

The result (an overweight body) justifies the original faulty idea (I'm no good, there must be something wrong with me), and this idea is further reinforced in your imagination. You become trapped in a vicious circle of non-constructive thought until a major life change pushes you out or you make a **decision** to pull yourself out.

> To free yourself from guilt, you must acknowledge the truth that you have not understood the power of your thoughts and feelings, nor realized the importance of adopting more constructive beliefs about yourself and your body.

Is it any wonder then, that you fail to lose weight when you have been innocently unaware of the cause of your problem? Is it your fault that you have failed when no one ever told you the correct way to use your tools in order to produce the result you want?

If you are miserable and unhappy with yourself or your body, you are surely using your tools incorrectly. It's unlikely, however, that you are doing it on purpose!

The next time your actions conflict with what you hope to accomplish, (like eating twice as much as you intended to eat) don't criticize yourself too harshly. Look for the reason why you behave this way and you will find it in the thoughts and feelings that preceded the action.

As you develop new habits of thinking, and use your imagination and emotions to support your desire, your actions will reflect these constructive thoughts and feelings as surely as they have reflected the old, self-critical ones.

Whether you are grossly overweight and angry at yourself or slightly overweight and frustrated for repeatedly failing to lose five pounds, there is no need to suffer any longer. Armed with the knowledge of the constructive use of your power and the **decision** and determination to apply it in the right direction, nothing can stop you now.

Part VI

---

8 Steps to Achieve and Maintain Your Ideal Weight

You are never given a wish without also being given the Power to make it true. You may have to work for it however.

--Richard Bach

Chapter 12

---

8 Steps
to Achieve and Maintain
Your Ideal Weight

The 8 Steps summarize some of the most important concepts presented in previous chapters. As you read the steps, you may discover that one or two of them have more meaning to you than others. Perhaps it represents an area in your life that needs your attention or needs to be healed. If so, you will want to start with the most meaningful step.

Begin by making a firm commitment to activate the power of that principle in your life. Then design a series of questions that will get your mind thinking about new possibilities for action.

For instance, if you feel particularly weak in the area of self-love and forgiveness (Step 6), you might ask:

How can I treat myself with more love and respect?

How can I feel more appreciation and gratitude for who I am right now?

What must I do in order to forgive myself?

What action can I take today to express appreciation and gratitude for myself and my body?

Or, if you need to develop trust in the wisdom of your inner self to guide you (Step 5), you might ask:

How can I develop trust in the wisdom of my inner self to guide me?

How does my subconscious mind assist me in other areas of my life?

What action can I take today to develop and express greater faith in my inner self?"

Make a commitment to ask yourself these questions every morning for the next four to six weeks. Ask each question again and again until you are satisfied with the answers you receive.

If you work with one step at a time, one day at a time, you will soon form new habits of thinking about yourself, your body, and your life situation. Constructive habits of thought and feeling lead to constructive action. Taking constructive action will bring you the results you want.

The 8 Steps—At a Glance

1

Acknowledge Your Power and Potential.

2

Take Back the Power You Have Given Away.

3

Take Control of Your Power Through Desire and Decision.

4

Let Go of the Problem: Focus Your Attention on Your Objectives—Not on the Obstacles In Your Way.

5

Trust Your Inner Self and Learn to Listen to Its Guidance.

6

Love, Forgive, and Accept Yourself and Your Body "As Is."

7

Take Possession of Your Desire in the Present: Act "As If" You are the Person You Want to Be.

8

Take Action on Every Level of Your Ability to Act: Mentally, Emotionally, and Physically.

Step 1

Acknowledge *Your Power and Potential.*

Your Mental, Emotional, and Physical Energy is Your Power.

You are a powerful person. You have the power of your will, thoughts, feelings, and physical actions. You have a mind and emotions with which to desire, dream, imagine, believe, choose, accept, reject, love, forgive, reason, decide, and so much more. You have a body that can walk, talk, run, dance, sing, and move in countless ways.

Each word describes a unique application of your energy. And each application of your energy produces a result. You can idle away your time and energy, spend it carelessly, or put it into forward gear and move swiftly toward your goal. You have mental, emotional, and physical energy with which to re-shape your body and create your life as you choose. This is your power. It is truly without limit.

Your Freedom of Expression is Your Potential.

Each moment of your life, you are faced with count-less choices. You must constantly choose how to spend your time and energy, and the choices you make determine the quality of your life.

In any given moment you are free to choose a new direction, a new desire, a new pattern for your thoughts and feelings to follow. You are free to express a new dimension of you: a different aspect of your personality, a renewed sense of strength and determination, a hidden skill or talent, or a new way of looking at the challenges in your life.

There's no need to travel the same old roads that lead to frustration and misery. You are endowed with the power of free will. This means that whatever you desire to be, to have, or to do is your choice. From this moment on, why not make a commitment to direct your energy—your thoughts, feelings and actions—toward being the person you always envisioned you would become "someday?" Why not decide to follow only those roads that lead to a brighter, fuller experience of life?

Your power and potential merely await your direction. But one thing is certain: you will direct and use them according to your understanding, according to your desire, intent and purpose, and according to your beliefs which underlie all your actions.

You cannot separate what you do from who you are, nor what you believe, and what you feel in your heart from what you create in both your outer environment and the health and condition of your body.

Take a moment each day to acknowledge the power and potential within you; to become aware of the many ways in which you are using your power constructively. Notice how you are free to choose the focus and direction of your conscious attention. Observe how your behavior follows the state of your mind and emotions.

Each day brings a new set of opportunities to renew your sense of purpose and find greater joy in living. Why not seize the opportunity to increase your personal power and unleash your potential?

If you will acknowledge your power and potential, you will gain a wonderful sense of control over the direction of your life. If you will feel grateful for the power and potential you do have, you will increase and expand it within you. And if you persist in applying your power wisely, you will know the joy of achieving your desire.

Step 2

T*ake Back the Power You Have Given Away.*

You Are Not a Victim of Your Environment.

You are the cause, the source and creator of your circumstances. As long as you have a mind to imagine, emotions to motivate, and a body to act, you are never helpless or powerless in the face of circumstance.

No environmental influence can prevent you from using your imagination to move your self into a better frame of mind, thereby improving the condition of your body. No situation is stronger than your inner will to focus your imagination and emotions on whatever you choose to think about.

This power belongs to you. Truly, no one is more responsible for your mental, emotional and physical behavior than you are. The choices you have made, have made you who you are today. The choices you are making today will determine who you are tomorrow.

If you are ready to choose a better tomorrow, you must take back the power you have given away. You give away your power when you believe in the opinions and importance of other people and outside forces *more* than you believe in yourself or your own body. Your mental and emotional energy may be wasted each day by the false belief that other things have more power than you do to define and direct your life.

In order to be fully empowered, you must take back the power you give to the opinions of others. Opinions are mere ideas about reality that cannot influence your own thoughts unless you allow them to. Instead of judging yourself by other people's standards of success and beauty, create your own standards that you will want to live by.

Take back the power you give to time as an obstacle to your success. Let go of your imaginary timetable as a means of weighing your success and gauging your accomplishment. Stop using time as a yardstick to measure your progress or to beat yourself up with. Deadlines and target dates can assist you when they inspire you, but not when they create anxiety and fear.

Take back the power you give to scientific studies and statistics that speak of your limited ability to achieve and maintain your ideal weight. Statistics often reflect and measure the attitude of the experimenter more than your chances for success. The inner wisdom that built your body from an embryo to an adult has a greater chance of healing you than modern science does. But you must ask the wisdom of your body for guidance and be willing to listen.

Take back the power you give to certain foods, weight charts, and meaningless numbers on the bathroom scale. Take a long, hard look at what each of these things can and cannot do for you, how they make you feel, and why you have given them any power or importance at all. Western culture places far too much emphasis on measuring the body's age, height, fat, and weight.

And finally, take back any power you have given to the past or the future. Stop expecting either of these aspects of time to rob you of your power to act in the present moment, in whatever manner you choose to act.

Take Responsibility for the Choices You Make.

Be willing to accept responsibility for your power, for the consequences of the choices you make each day. Once you accept responsibility for the results of your actions, you will know you have the power to change those results. You will realize that you can take your life into your own hands, redirect your energy toward constructive activity, and change the entire course of your life.

Instead of blaming other people or outer circumstances for becoming who you are, search within for reasons why you have chosen this course of action. There you will find the answers to your misery and your joy, to your failures and your accomplishments. You are the one who must direct your energy constructively or forever suffer the consequences.

Step 3

Take Control of Your Power Through Desire and Decision.

A Clear Desire Activates Your Imagination and Emotions.

Everything you accomplish begins with desire. You must have the desire or intent to do something, the will to direct your actions toward accomplishing a particular result.

A clear desire acts as a blueprint for creating and maintaining the results you want. It enables your imagination to fill in the details of your plan and helps you attract and find whatever resources you will need to create it.

Desire is also the wellspring of emotion; as you visualize the elements of your desire and dwell upon them in your mind, you generate more energy and momentum to move you toward achieving it.

Creating your ideal body-weight begins with desire. It is a choice among many choices you can make and other things you can do with your time and energy. Only you have the power to say "I *want* to do this for me. I *can* become the slender, healthy person I want to become. I *will* do what it takes to achieve this instead of maintaining my present condition. I *must* change who I am and become the person I want to be. I deserve to experience the joy this will bring me."

A Firm Decision Paves the Way for Action.

Once you are clear about what you want, you must make a decision to have it. Decision plants your desire firmly in mind, and puts an end to doubt or vacillation among the many choices you can make. Once again, if you have conflicting desires you must clearly decide between one or the other. Otherwise, your desire to achieve your ideal weight will remain a mere "wish," unable to generate or sustain the emotional energy you will need to achieve it.

E-*moti*-ons act as the *moti*-vating force to propel you into *moti*-on toward the attainment of your desire. Together, desire (conscious choice) and decision (emotional commitment to obtain it) produce powerful results. Decision generates the emotional conviction or belief that your desire is possible and paves the way for action to follow.

The world is a storehouse of treasures. It is willing and capable of supplying your every need, want and desire. But it is up to you to select what you want and decide that you will have it. You must exercise your freedom to choose from among an infinite number of possibilities, those objects, events and experiences that suit you.

In other words, the desire to be, to have or do must come from within you. It must be a thought-feeling that moves you into action, something you believe will add to your life. Once you have a clear desire and make the decision to have it, you will also find it easier to believe you can achieve it.

Decide now to set a clear direction for your imagination and emotions to follow. Use the power of your imagination to clarify your desire to become who you want to be. Make a decision (a firm emotion-backed commitment) to direct your mental, emotional and physical efforts toward being this person.

Then trust that your desire is on its way by turning your thoughts toward other things. Expect that it will soon be yours and it will be.

Step 4

Let Go of the Problem:
Focus Your Attention on Your Objectives—
Not on the Obstacles in Your Way.

Dwelling Upon Your Problem Will Only Increase It.

Every moment you spend concentrating upon a problem increases its power and importance in your life and causes it to persist. You merely add more energy and give more life to a problem by focusing your attention upon it! If you will forget about your weight problem or refuse to regard it as an obstacle, it will lose its power to threaten your joy and success.

Whenever you concentrate on how miserable you feel about yourself or the condition of your body, you increase your opportunities for remaining that way forever. As you dwell upon failure, lack and limitation, you live and relive these in your mind until they are all you can perceive in your experience.

If you believe and constantly think you have a weight problem, you will have, because your beliefs are like powerful magnets that draw the elements of your thought to you. A belief that you have this "problem" fills your mind with other thoughts, feelings and images you associate with this condition. This belief (emotion-backed image) will continue to attract similar thoughts that are readily accepted because they are in agreement with your belief! How can you expect to behave like a slender person when the belief that you have a weight problem pervades your thoughts and feelings?

This is why you must let go of the problem and concentrate upon your objectives—upon your desire, intent and purpose—instead of the obstacles in your way. A mind that dwells upon obstacles and problems will also find it difficult, if not impossible, to perceive solutions. Only by releasing the problem from your thought can you free your mind from images of what you don't want and enable solutions to appear. Silence your mind from the fear and frustration of your problem, and suddenly you will become receptive to ideas that can set you free.

Turn Your Attention Toward Other Things That Interest You.

The imagination and willpower are related. If you attempt to use willpower to block a thought from your mind, it brings it into your imagination. To will yourself to stop wanting a certain food brings an image of the food to your conscious attention, giving it more energy and power. This generates more anxiety, and you become locked in a vicious circle of futile attempts to block it from your mind.

When you want to release a problem, make a decision to focus your attention in a new direction and think about other things that give you joy. As undesirable thoughts or images come to mind, use your will and imagination to visualize the process of releasing them. Generate the emotion opposite of the one you feel and recognize these thoughts as faulty ideas that are no longer a part of you. Forgive yourself for having them, and simply release them from your mind.

With the power of your will and imagination, focus your attention on having the body you do want instead of the one you don't. Dwell upon your new image, your blessings and strengths, until you feel completely grateful for them.

If you refuse to give a problem your attention, time, energy or emotion, it will eventually cease to exist. Sooner or later the old ideas and images fade away from lack of attention. So why not refuse to focus on food, fat, flaws or failure, and dwell upon thoughts that inspire you instead? Keep your mind attuned to your purpose, your desire and your

Delete deprivation.

destination. Like a water pitcher with only so much space to fill, you can displace non-constructive habits of thought by filling your mind with constructive ones.

It is your choice to be free of your problem with food, fat, and failure to lose weight by dieting. You *will* be free as soon as you choose to be.

Step 5

Trust Your Inner Self and Learn to Listen to Its Guidance.

Conscious Thought Sets the Direction; Inner Wisdom Takes You There.

When you decide to walk across a room, you don't need to consciously command every nerve and muscle involved in the action. Your subconscious mind accepts your desire and decision and spontaneously performs millions of calculations necessary for putting your body into motion.

Your conscious mind holds the image of your destination—where it is you want to go, or what it is you want to accomplish. As long as you know where you want to go and are determined to get there, the subconscious mind carries out your desire automatically.

You don't need to understand how it does this, but you do need to trust that it will. It is similar to driving a car: you don't need to understand how a car works in order to drive one, but you do need to know what direction to point it in. In the use of your inner power and potential, the conscious mind is like the steering mechanism, setting the direction or choosing a course of action, while the subconscious mind is like the engine with the power you need to take you there.

The inner self is willing and able to do the vast majority of the work for us, but the problem lies in our lack of trust in our inner ability to take us where we want to go. We doubt its abilities because we don't understand how it will perform its miracles.

Have you ever noticed how effortlessly your subconscious mind drives your car while you are deeply engrossed in a daydream? There's no need to pay constant attention to how or where you are going. There's no need to struggle or strive to control every action you take.

The same applies to achieving your ideal weight. Simply use your conscious mind to set a direction, to form a clear vision of who you want to become and what you want to look like. Then expect and allow your subconscious mind to guide you toward your ideal image.

Trust Your Inner Wisdom to Guide You Toward Success.

Your subconscious mind knows exactly what to do and will operate in mysterious and miraculous ways to bring about your desire, if you will only get out of its way and believe in it; if you will cut out the noise and confusion of your conscious mind and listen for its guidance; if you will hear the messages coming from your body and follow your intuitive impulses toward action.

You must develop faith in your inner wisdom, knowledge and innate ability to achieve your desire. If you can trust an airline pilot you've never seen before with your life—if you can trust your dentist, doctor, or the cooks in the restaurants you eat in—you can learn to trust that part of your mind that keeps your heart beating and manages to keep you alive.

The inner self creates the outer self—naturally and spontaneously. You enable it to create your finest image by turning your attention toward other things and trusting your inner wisdom to restore good health and the weight that is ideal for you.

Step 6

Love, Forgive, and Accept Yourself and Your Body "As Is."

Self-love Will Open the Door to Your Desire.

Self-love begins with self-respect. If you believe you are attractive, intelligent, witty, wonderful or generally worthy of the best life has to offer, you can consider yourself fortunate. But if the ideas you have adopted about your self or your body define you as fat, ugly, stupid or unworthy of love and respect, you have some work to do.

It takes self-love and self-acceptance to expand your mind and emotions and open the door to your desire. How can you receive your desire if you close your mind, shut down your emotions, and refuse to gratefully acknowledge or accept it? You must love and respect yourself *before* you can receive the joy your desire will bring you.

You must love yourself enough to adopt a new set of beliefs that define who you are. You must love yourself enough to adopt a new perspective, a new awareness of the riches in your life, of the beauty of your character, of whatever wealth and positive attributes you own. You must love yourself enough to make time to do what you love to do. If you will treat yourself with love and respect, you will become a happier, self-fulfilled person. As you become a happier, self-fulfilled person, you will not only have more love to give to others, but will attract more opportunities to live life to the fullest.

It is also essential to love and respect your body no matter how it may appear to you in the moment. Your body has as much right to your love and acceptance as you give the trees, the moon, animals or other people. Only by loving your body "as is" can you open your mind to the positive attributes of your physical form, release your excess weight, and make it possible to become who you want to be.

Your physical appearance will naturally change as you change your innermost thoughts and feelings, not by force or an effort of willpower, but by release of your inner potential and acceptance of your right to joy and fulfillment.

You don't have to earn your right to happiness or give up something you love in order to have what you want. You deserve all the joy your heart can hold and you don't have to give up anything. You do need to willingly receive more of life's blessings. And you do need to love, accept, and honor your self and your body.

Forgiveness Opens the Door to Love.

To forgive yourself is like opening a channel for more life to flow through you. Self-forgiveness releases non-constructive thoughts and feelings and allows new ones to flood in. It frees your mind and emotions from anxiety and self-critical thoughts, and enables you to feel worthy. And as you feel a greater sense of self-worth, you will naturally find it easier to achieve your ideal weight.

You must learn to forgive, accept and feel good about who and what you are in this moment. Not who you were yesterday, five years ago or last month. Not who you will become tomorrow, but who you are right now.

If you cannot accept the integrity and worth of your being right now, you will find it difficult to imagine what it feels like to have your desire. Only by accepting your desire in your imagination do you prepare yourself to receive it in form. Ultimately, self-love, acceptance and forgiveness will make it easier to go where you want to go, and also make it possible to stay.

Step 7

Take Possession of Your Desire in the Present: Act "As If" You are the Person You Want to Be.

The Present Moment is the Only Moment You Can Act In.

Your power to think, feel, and act is in the present moment. It is the only moment you will ever have to think differently, feel differently and act differently. Therefore, why not use the present moment to imagine, feel and act "as if" you are the person you desire to be?

Within your imagination, you have the ability to experience an event well before it occurs in reality. Time doesn't have to elapse before you can feel what it's like to experience your desire. Whatever you can imagine and believe you can be, you can be. And as you practice and pretend to be who you want to be, you become that person.

You may think that excess fat stands in your way of feeling self-confident and physically attractive. If so, you haven't realized that in order to be these things, you must accept the idea that they are already yours. Acceptance is a confirmation of your belief; it means you are mentally prepared and emotionally open to act upon and receive your desire.

Again, you can only have what you are willing to accept and receive, and you must first receive it within your imagination. As you form a clear image and get in touch with the emotional elements of your desire, you increase your belief in its attainment; your enthusiasm rises and you are motivated to take the actions that will create your vision.

Your mind, emotions, and body are in a constant state of change. Since change is a necessary part of living, why not welcome and direct it instead of fearing or resisting it? You can generate constructive change by putting your creative power in forward gear. By thinking and feeling and acting as if you already are the person you desire to be.

No one else can offer you self-respect and self-confidence or force you to change your self-perception. You must do this for yourself. If you truly want to feel love, acceptance, joy and relief from the burden of your weight problem, why wait until some distant time in the future? You can enjoy these feelings right now in your imagination. You can allow yourself to receive them in your heart as well as your head, as a state of being that you not only desire, but deserve to enjoy.

But you can't keep projecting that state of being into the future, to some vague, indefinite hour when you will have finally arrived. Success is realized one step at a time. You must act as if because "someday" never comes; there are only more moments just like the one you are living.

Forget the Mistakes of the Past, Apply Your Power in the Present, and the Future Will Take Care of Itself.

You are not a victim of past events, even though you may allow them to intrude upon your happiness and peace of mind in the present. You bring them into your life and give them power by choosing to focus upon them. By turning your attention toward events that no longer have the power to harm you, you waste valuable mental, emotional, and physical energy that could be better spent on constructive action in the present moment.

Make a decision right now to use your thought-energy wisely: decide who you really are, what is a part of your character and what is not. Listen to your inner dialogue and begin to recognize any false and degrading opinions you've accepted about yourself or your body. Refuse to accept or dwell upon ideas which do not fit your own ideal image.

Instead of searching your memory for the reasons to explain your failures, recall and retrieve your past successes. It makes little difference whether you have gained weight because of emotional trauma, parental pressure to clean your plate at dinner-time, boredom, self-hatred, or a combination of all of these. How you arrived at your present state of mind and physical condition is not as important as making the choice to do something about it.

Right now, in this moment, you have the power to change your perception of your self and your body. Take this moment and live it wisely. Use it to give yourself the love you have been wanting and the love you have always deserved.

Step 8

Take Action on Every Level of Your Ability to Act: *Mentally, Emotionally, and Physically.*

Align the Powers of Your Mind, Emotions and Body.

You are more than a physical body. You are a spiritual, mental, emotional and physical being. If you are determined to succeed this time, you cannot expect to focus your attention on a single aspect of your life while ignoring the reality of another. Your success will depend upon how you direct, focus and apply all of your energy—not just a part of it.

In other words, you cannot ignore the state of your mind and emotions while you try to sweat or starve the fat from your body. Nor can you sit idly and attempt to think yourself thin without expending effort on the physical level. Your desire for a more slender body must also be converted into physical action.

Consider a more simple desire: You want to grow a flower garden. No one can give you this desire; the motivation, intent and purpose must originate and emanate from within you. You are the primary source of energy for your desire to be transformed from a thought to a physical reality.

You will need a clear intent and purpose to cultivate a particular type of flower. If you aren't clear about what you want to grow and why you want it, you may find all sorts of weeds popping up around you.

As you imagine the enjoyment your garden will bring you with the confident expectation of receiving it, your desire will build within you, until one day it urges you to take the physical action necessary to create it.

You will use the physical energy of your body to plant the garden, but mental energy will be required to imagine it in the first place, to plan the garden and direct your body to plant the seeds and keep the garden free from weeds and pests.

Emotional energy is another necessary ingredient. You will need to love and nurture your garden with care. Yet without the mysterious source of spiritual energy which enables you to think, feel and act, and which transforms the sun, soil and water into a flower, growing your garden would be impossible.

Now compare this simple desire with your desire to achieve and maintain your ideal weight without dieting. (This too, is a simple desire, but we make it more difficult by believing that it is.)

No one can give you the desire to change your physical form. The motivation, intent and purpose to direct your energy toward this result must originate and emanate from within you.

You must nourish this desire and imagine all the benefits it will bring you with the confident expectation of receiving them. If you don't expect to succeed, you may find all sorts of excuses popping up in your mind to explain why you can't enjoy this experience right now.

The expectation of receiving your desire causes you to see the ways in which your body has already begun to respond, to find what beauty there is in its current form, instead of focusing on the beauty it lacks. As you trust and expect to achieve your desire, your actions will support and move you toward your desire.

You will need to love, praise and nurture the creative energy within you instead of expecting it to fail you. You wouldn't criticize a flower for its unique form of beauty, so you must realize how ridiculous it is to criticize your own.

Cultivate Patience.

You will need to cultivate patience and expect the magic to happen by itself. You wouldn't think of demanding that a seed perform its miracle within a certain amount of time, so why make this demand upon yourself? If you wouldn't sit impatiently watching your garden for signs of growth, why should you scrutinize your body every day expecting it to perform its miracles as you watch?

Whether you are waiting for a flower to grow or a pot of water to boil, it will seem to take forever. But one day you awake to find a flower in your garden that has magically appeared overnight.

And so it is with the transformation of your body. One day, you will look in the mirror and see the inner magic you have brought into being reflected in the image of your body. You will realize that the outer image of your body is indeed a reflection of the inner images you hold within your mind. Without conscious striving or struggle you will have achieved the weight that is ideal for you, and will easily maintain it forever.

ACTION GUIDE

Tools and Techniques to Apply Your Power Constructively

If you would like a beautiful garden, you had better eliminate the weeds first.

--Meditations of Rumi

Chapter 13

Exposing Self-Limiting Beliefs

A belief is an emotion-backed idea we accept as truth about reality, ourself or our body. Beliefs are often mere opinions about reality—not necessarily the truth—but they appear to be true precisely because they color and filter our perception. In other words, beliefs cause us to think, feel and act in ways that help to bring about the ideas we believe in.

If you will examine the contents of your mind, you may find a number of self-limiting beliefs that can be replaced with self-liberating ones. Of course, you will need a desire to do so, and then back up your desire with mental and physical effort, but it can truly be a rewarding as well as enlightening experience.

Are you ready to take an objective look at your thoughts and feelings? Create a separate page in your journal with these headings and enter the date on each page:

1. **Beliefs, Thoughts, and Feelings About Myself and My Body"**

2. **Beliefs, Thoughts, and Feelings About Food and Weight Loss**

3. **Beliefs, Thoughts, and Feelings About My Life Situation**

Where are your current beliefs, thoughts and feelings leading you? What kind of beliefs, thoughts and feelings will bring you to your destination once and for all?

Listed below are a series of questions that will help you find out. It may take you some time to answer them, but in case you doubt whether it's worth the effort, don't!

Your answers will act as important clues to your success. Later on, you may want to take your answers to these questions and turn them into affirmations that will help you reach your destination.

Beliefs, Thoughts, and Feelings About Myself and My Body

- What kind of things did you think about as you got dressed this morning?

- What else do you think about every day—particularly when your mind is free to wander (as you shower, dress, gaze in the mirror, prepare a meal, drive somewhere, before going to bed)?

- What do you tell yourself about the way you look?

- What kind of person are you? Describe some of your strengths and weaknesses.

- What do you believe has been responsible for your gaining excess weight? (Heredity, poor eating habits, lack of exercise, lack of self-discipline, social circumstances or environment, emotional problems, physiological problems, some combination of all of these)

- Do you believe you have what it takes to overcome the obstacles you've just listed?

    Look at your answers to the questions above. What type of feelings accompany your typical thoughts?

- How do you expect to feel about yourself once you've reached your desired weight?

- Do you expect to fit in the same clothes you used to wear or are you looking forward to buying new clothes?

- How would you describe your predominant feelings? Are you totally miserable emotionally? Can you sense any particular mood that prevails throughout a typical day?

- How do you feel about who you are and what you look like? Do you feel thoroughly disgusted? Frustrated? Angry or disappointed with yourself?

- How do you feel about the human body in general?

- Do you believe the human body is truly a miraculous creation?

- What do you think of the body's ability to heal itself?

- Do you feel that the human body is endowed with the inner wisdom to maintain optimum health? Why or why not?

- Can the human body be trusted to tell us when we're hungry? Can it be trusted to tell us when to stop eating?

After you have answered the questions above, reword them to read *my body* instead of *the human body*. Contrast your feelings about your own body with your feelings and beliefs about the human body in general. Include these comments in your journal under the heading "Beliefs, thoughts, and feelings about myself and my body."

Beliefs, Thoughts, and Feelings About Food and Weight Loss

- What are your habitual thoughts about food?

- Do you constantly think about food and dieting?

- What do you say to others about your weight?

- What do you tell others about your plans and aspirations?

- When you think about food, how do you feel?

- How do you feel about your previous attempts (and/or failures) to lose weight and keep it off?

- Do you expect to gain weight from eating certain fattening foods?

- What are your expectations with regard to dieting?

- When you go on a diet, do you expect to lose a certain amount of weight within a week, a month or a year?

- Do you start each diet with the expectation of success or the expectation of failure?

- What is your attitude toward losing weight?

- Are you sick and tired of thinking about it?

- What do you believe is the best way to achieve and maintain your ideal weight?

- Do you believe losing weight is difficult because it's impossible to avoid eating food?

Beliefs, Thoughts, and Feelings About My Life Situation

- What images and ideas occupy your mind as you go about your daily affairs at home or at work?

- What do you say about others in your life?

- How do you feel about others in your life? Do you feel they support you in your efforts to change yourself and your body?

- How do you expect others to react once you've reached your desired weight? Will they be pleased? Jealous? Will they resent you or praise you?

- How do you feel about the way you spend most of your time? Are you happy with what you are doing? Do you feel self-fulfilled or a gnawing sense of lacking and want?

- Once you've lost the weight you want to lose, what other benefits do you expect to enjoy besides a slender body? (Attention or approval from others, an increase in your salary, greater self-confidence . . .)

- Do you believe someone else is even partly responsible for your weight gain or inability to maintain your ideal weight?

- Is there anything or anyone in your current situation that makes it difficult or impossible for you to reach your goal?

Listed below are some of the typical beliefs, thoughts, feelings and expectations of a frustrated dieter. Do any of these sound familiar? Do you agree with any of these statements? If so, include them in your journal.

I'm fat.
I'm ugly.
Certain foods make me gain weight.
I'll never have a slender body.
I need food to fill an emotional void in my life.
I don't deserve to be happy or successful.
I have to lose weight before others will accept me.
I don't deserve love. I'm not a lovable person.
I'm disgusting—out of control.
I'm a failure.
The only way to lose weight is to go on a diet.
I'm always hungry.
I constantly think about food.
I'm angry and frustrated, and I feel helpless to
    overcome my weight problem.
I don't have any self-discipline.
I can't maintain a consistent exercise program.
I'm a slave to physical gratification.
I have an addictive personality.
I love to eat.

It's too difficult to overcome the childhood programming and self-destructive behavior patterns I've adopted. I would have to be in therapy for years.

I can't stick to a diet or any plans for losing weight. I always give in to temptation and allow myself "just one" cookie and "just one" piece of bread when I know I shouldn't.

I am a procrastinator. I tell myself I'll start my diet tomorrow or next Monday instead of starting today.

Something within me causes me to fail again and again. It works against me no matter how hard I try.

I guess I want to be fat to avoid other people.

I can't break any of my bad habits: I eat when I'm full, I eat when I'm watching TV, I eat when I have nothing better to do.

I want to eat *more* than I want a beautiful, slim figure.

I'm not willing to pay the price, to make the sacrifice I need to make in order to lose weight.

I have a slow metabolism. Other people eat the same amount of food that I eat and never gain any weight.

I don't care anymore. No one loves me anyway. What's the use?

I love to eat because it gives me pleasure; its fun and enjoyable and I don't want to give it up.

I eat whenever I'm happy, bored, lonely, or feeling anxious and upset.

I always eat too fast (too much, too late at night . . .)

I can't give up bread and butter. I crave starches, chocolate, and other foods with a certain taste and texture.

I'm obsessed with food.

I think about eating all the time.

I can't control myself around food—it controls me.

Losing weight requires discipline, self-control and a lot of willpower. I don't have enough of these qualities.

Losing weight requires patience and persistence, which I don't have.

I travel all the time. I have to entertain clients and eat out at restaurants. The portions served are usually more than I need, and I don't want to waste the food or my money.

My husband (roommate, mother. . .) likes to bake. This makes it impossible for me to stick to my diet.

I have to cook dinner for my family. When I cook, I also have to taste everything.

Part of my job is to attend a lot of social gatherings and parties where food is served.

My social life is very active and there is always food at social gatherings. It's rude not to eat what the host has prepared for you.

Take the next fifteen minutes to review what you have written under each of the headings. Examine each idea and ask yourself if it rings true. **Question any idea that makes you feel bad, guilty, undeserving or frustrated.** Then write a counter-argument to any thought that does not empower or inspire you to become the person you want to be.

Think about any faulty beliefs until you can discover a new way to look at it. If necessary, go back to Chapter 12 and review the 8 Steps until you have a different perspective. Below are some examples to get you started.

I know something is wrong with me but I don't know what.

I *do know* what is wrong with me. I have forgotten how to have a natural and healthy relationship with food and must adopt new attitudes about it.

I feel anxious and frustrated. I want to lose weight but can't seem to do it.

I *can* do it. I can change my emotions by changing my mental focus. I now understand how my thoughts, feelings, beliefs and expectations create the reality I experience.

I don't have the discipline or motivation to make a permanent change.

I *do have* the discipline and motivation I need. I have all the power I will ever need to create my desire right now.

I inherited a slow metabolism from my parents and grandparents.

Perhaps I have also inherited their beliefs and attitudes toward food. If I change my beliefs and my attitude toward food, my actions will change and so will my body.

The Side Effects of Feeling Fat

When you don't feel good about who you are or where you're going, it's difficult to find happiness in other areas of your life. Your emotional well-being affects your social life as well as your physical health.

There can be many unpleasant side effects of feeling fat. As a frustrated dieter you may feel out of touch with who you want to be and seemingly powerless to change it. Can you relate to any of these feelings?

Self-directed anger
Anxiety and frustration
Confusion
Depression
Discouragement and despair

Guilt
Lack of hope
Lack of self-confidence
Lack of self-esteem
Lack of trust in your inner self and in your body
Lack of energy and enthusiasm
Lack of approval from others
Lack of acknowledgment, love and
    appreciation from others
Feeling helpless or powerless to change the situation
Feeling "out of it," a social outcast
Feeling ugly and unattractive
Self-consciousness
Self-contempt or self-hatred

You can use any of these negative emotions to lead you back to the belief that underlies it. For example, if you find yourself suddenly feeling guilty or discouraged, ask yourself these questions:

"What thoughts just preceded this feeling?"
"What do I believe about this situation that causes me to feel this way?"

Search for the inner dialogue that just took place. Then write it down and take a look at it. Don't judge yourself for having these thoughts; merely release them and forgive yourself for misdirecting your mental and emotional energy.

Remember, the beliefs and thoughts you entertain about yourself, your body, and your life situation are not necessarily the truth. Recognize the ones that are not and release them before they affect your mood or your behavior.

Chapter 14

Building Upon Constructive Beliefs and Success

Now that you are aware of some of the faulty beliefs you have been harboring, it is time to acknowledge the beliefs that have served you well.

Take a moment to think of something in your life you are pleased with—some accomplishment, however small, that you are proud of (even if it is only learning how to ride a bicycle). Then take another moment to consider the type of beliefs that preceded your success. What kind of thoughts, feelings, and expectations did you experience as a result of your **belief** in your ability to achieve the result you wanted?

Whatever your profession or position in life, you have put a lot of thought and feeling into producing these results. If you are an accomplished musician, for instance, how did you become one? Not everyone can play a musical instrument, so there must be something you have done to achieve this success.

Did you have a strong **desire** to play music? Was your desire backed by the **belief** that you could develop your talent? Was this belief eventually strong enough to lead you to purchase an instrument and motivate you to spend endless hours practicing or playing for the fun of it? Did you **feel** enthusiastic about playing or listening to music? When you practiced a new tune, did you **expect** to be able to play it well? Did this expectation urge you to practice it over and over again until you finally had it down, but were completely tired of hearing it?

Perhaps you are a great tennis player, cook, doctor, nurse or mother. How did you achieve this success? Look for some of the beliefs, thoughts and feelings preceding the actions you took to get there and you will find them. Success is best achieved when constructive energy is persistently applied with the hope and expectation of success.

Again, this doesn't mean you never entertained a single doubt in your mind while working toward your objectives. It only means that the sum of your faith was greater than your fear and doubt. Faith is what kept you going when the going got rough. It over-powered your fear and overcame the obstacles. It gave you the energy, strength and determination to persist until you were well beyond defeat.

The same faith and beliefs you have used successfully in other areas of your life, at any age, can work for you right now.

Recall what you thought or expected to achieve as you worked toward the objectives you have attained. Use your imagination to get in touch with the feeling of accomplishment and success, then transfer these thoughts and feelings to your current situation. Experience what it feels like to achieve your ideal weight.

Every task undertaken requires thought, action and trust in your ability to do it. You would never learn how to read, ride a bike or drive a car if you lived in perpetual fear of failure or doubted your ability to succeed. It takes courage, faith, desire, persistence and effort to learn how to read, drive a car or ride a bike—and it takes these same things to become who you want to be, in thought, in feeling, and in action.

Create a separate page in your journal with the following headings:

My Accomplishments and Successes
(Large and Small)

Beliefs, Thoughts, Feelings and Expectations
That Have Served Me Well

Now set aside at least one-half hour to think and write about the above headings. Start with the result you achieved such as learning how to drive a car. Then consider the kind of beliefs, thoughts, feelings and expectations that prompted your actions: "I can do it; this will be easy; learning how to drive means having more fun and more freedom; I can't wait to get my license; I'll be able to go anywhere. I felt enthusiastic, excited, and confident that I would learn how to drive. I expected to succeed, and kept taking action toward my goal until I did. The result? I learned how to drive a car."

Chapter 15

Constructive Use of Your Imagination and Emotions

Have you ever watched a small child playing with a toy? If you take away their toy without giving them another, they are likely to scream and cry. Yet if you replace the toy with something new, their attention will happily turn to the new object.

The mind and imagination need something to occupy it. Like a child with a new toy, you will need to replace your non-constructive habits of thinking with something new. You will need to feed your mind with images of what you want— allowing it to wander and play and focus on those images.

155

You may want to create a colorful and visual wishbook for this purpose—cutting out pictures of what you want and pasting or taping them inside a notebook.

The mind loves to play with images and ideas. In fact, everyone likes to daydream now and then—wondering what something would be like, imagining a pleasurable event, trying out an experience, or envisioning a new way of doing something.

Using your imagination should come easy, because you use it spontaneously all the time. However, thoughts flow so effortlessly from one image-idea to another that the entire process of imagining and visualizing is often taken for granted. For this reason you must make a conscious decision to direct your imagination toward a new way of thinking, feeling and doing.

Take a moment to imagine biting into an apple. What does it taste like? What does it feel like? Do you like the sensation? Does it make you want to eat an apple right now?

Now imagine biting into a lemon. What does it taste like? What does it feel like? What differences do you notice about these two imagined events?

In this same playful way, you can use your imagination and emotions to:

(1) Replace non-constructive habits with constructive ones.

(2) Get in touch with a feeling of gratitude and the confident expectation of success.

(3) Develop respect and love for your body as it is.

(4) Internalize each of the 8 Steps to Achieve and Maintain Your Ideal Weight.

Let's use your imagination and emotions to consider the 8 Steps presented in Chapter 12.

Step 1 *Acknowledge Your Power and Potential.*

IMAGINE your mind with an invisible cable that links it to a universal mind, like a computer terminal linked to a giant mainframe. Now tap into its limitless power, call upon its resources and re-program your mind with new ideas and information. Imagine the joy of creating new patterns of thought, feeling and action. Ask any question you might have and **expect** to get an intelligent answer. It knows all, and because you are linked to it, you have access to its wisdom and knowledge.

Step 2 *Take Back the Power You have Given Away.*

IMAGINE going into a storehouse of thoughts. Surrounding you are thoughts of every color in the rainbow stored in large glass jars. Look around at all the colors, shapes and sizes of thoughts. Notice how vibrant and clear some of them are and how others are muddy and dark. Which ones will you choose for yourself? Select them carefully; they are the magnets that you will use to attract your desires. Which ones are you willing to try on and keep? These will paint the landscape of your life.

Step 3 *Take Control of Your Power through Desire and Decision.*

IMAGINE that you want to memorize a telephone number. First you must have the desire to memorize it; then you must decide that you will. Focus your attention and form a clear picture of the number in your mind, then decide to commit it to memory so you won't have to look it up each time you need it. You can use this same process to create other things you wish to have or be: desire (a clear mental image of what you want) and decision (emotional commitment, intensity of purpose) are at the root of every successful action.

Step 4   Let go of the Problem: Focus Your Attention on Your Objectives—Not on the Obstacles in Your Way.

IMAGINE your weight "problem" as a game of tug-of-war that you are playing with yourself. Feel yourself struggling in both directions. Then imagine letting go of the problem, so that it can no longer play or tug at you. Now you have rendered it powerless to affect your joy and success.

IMAGINE placing all of your thoughts and feelings upon a scale. On one side are constructive thoughts and light, joyful feelings; on the other side are self-critical thoughts and heavy, fearful feelings. Now balance your thoughts and feelings in your favor. As in a set of scales or on a seesaw, imagine placing yourself on the side of the positive image you wish to create. Now concentrate on being that person.

IMAGINE your thoughts as a constant stream of energy floating by. Be on the look out for any self-defeating thoughts that come along. Imagine the energy in these thoughts flowing through you and passing by. The energy of self-destructive thoughts dissipates or dies out from lack of interest and attention. Let it go— allow it to be free to create something else in the universe. Release it with a fond farewell saying, "So long, thank you for helping me to understand how my thoughts create my body's image. Now you can go." Don't judge or try to stop self-destructive thoughts; merely observe them as they come to mind and then imagine them floating downstream. Imagine them like a friend whom you have outgrown; it is time to move on. There won't be any pain in this departure—only new-found energy and joy.

IMAGINE your desire is to become a seasoned tennis player. As you dwell on all the things you are supposed to do when you serve the ball, you increase your skill and gain the confidence you need to perform as a pro. As a professional athlete, you understand the power of the will and imagination. When you rehearse your performance, you refuse to let your conscious, reasoning mind get in the way by focusing on the net, your opponent, the position of the sun or other potential obstacles. You have been trained to focus your attention on your purpose, upon the direction in which you choose to hit the ball. And you also know how to monitor your progress toward your ideal weight. You concentrate your attention on what you do right each day.

Step 5   Trust Your Inner Self and Learn to Listen to Its Guidance.

IMAGINE making a decision to walk across the room. What do you focus on? Do you look at each piece of furniture you can possibly bump into or trip over? Or do you look at your destination and walk with faith that each step brings you closer to the other side of the room? Now imagine that you want to "move" your mind from one frame of reference to another, from one kind of perspective to another—from frustration and despair to joy and enthusiasm. Do you freeze with fear and begin to doubt that you have what it takes to succeed? Are you allowing your imagination to conjure up reasons to explain or justify why you can't make it? If so, begin once more with faith this time.

IMAGINE that you are an inseparable part of a vast river of life-energy, flowing gracefully and deliberately onward. There is no need to cling to the banks of the river or hold on to faulty, self-limiting beliefs that slow you down. Imagine yourself letting go of the banks of the river and trusting the river of life to carry you effortlessly toward your destination.

Step 6   Love, Forgive, and Accept Yourself and Your Body "As Is."

IMAGINE entering a giant store filled with gems. Before you is a vast selection of diamonds, emeralds, and precious gemstones too numerous for you to take one of each. You must choose from among this assortment, make your purchase and enjoy its beauty. See yourself standing there in awe and wonderment. Are you wishing you could have it all but feeling that you don't deserve any? Now see yourself making a selection and wearing the gemstone on a chain around your neck. **Feel** its magical healing power drawing out your inner beauty and magnifying the love you feel for yourself and others.

IMAGINE sitting before a large feast of food. See yourself selecting only those foods that your body needs for optimum health and vitality. Because you care about yourself and your body, you naturally choose what is truly good for you. As you imagine this kind of relationship with food, you reinforce and support this quality as a part of your self-image. The next time a situation arises that calls for this new habit of action, you will behave in the manner that you have practiced in your imagination.

Step 7 Take Possession of Your Desire in the Present: Act "As If."

IMAGINE looking into a full-length mirror. Envision your body as you would like it to look. Feel what it's like to be lighter and smaller all over. Now begin to act "as if" you are the slender person you want to be. Get in touch with your slender self and have a conversation with him or her. Imagine what others will say to you when they see you. Accept their compliments and admiration.

Step 8 Take Action On Every Level of Your Ability to Act: Mentally, Emotionally, and Physically.

IMAGINE each new thought you have as a seed containing only the potential for full expression. Every thought you "plant" must have certain conditions to produce new growth, to reach maturity and become firmly rooted in your life. Who you want to be exists first as an idea, it is born or "seeded" in your mind and grows according to the mental, emotional and physical energy you give it everyday.

Imagine your habitual thoughts flourishing as you give them your attention. Visualize your ideal body in your imagination and feel how grateful you are. Imagine taking whatever action you can to support and nurture this vision. Now **feel** this seed you have planted actually growing stronger everyday, attracting all the elements it will need to fulfill your desire.

Chapter 16

Affirmations to Increase Your Power and Release Your Potential

To affirm is to make a positive statement that something is true. Affirmations are bold and positive declarations that can serve to make a feeling-image "firm" within your mind. And as you make it firm within your mind, your actions will naturally follow.

Use affirmations to change the focus of your mind. Use them to open your awareness to your power and to release your potential. Stated often, affirmations will help you replace non-constructive inner dialogue with constructive ideas that will inspire and guide you toward success.

After reading the following affirmations, select those that have special meaning to you and copy them into your journal. You may want to write your own or change the words slightly to create more emotional impact and meaning. Then set aside a time every morning and evening to say them out loud with as much feeling and sincerity that you can generate.

Repetition is a key to making these constructive thoughts and feelings your own. But more important is the imagination and emotion you put into your words as you speak them. Ultimately this is the power that produces inner change.

Step 1

I acknowledge my power and potential.

> I acknowledge the power of my imagination and emotions.
>
> I have the power to take constructive action.
>
> I am free to choose my thoughts and the focus of my attention.
>
> I am free to be whomever I want to be.
>
> I use my power wisely.
>
> My power increases with each effort I make to use it.
>
> I have everything I need to be successful.
>
> I believe in my worth and value as a person.
>
> I believe in me.

Step 2

I take back the power I have given to food.

I take back the power I have given to other people and outer circumstances.

> I am responsible for the state of my mind and emotions.
>
> I am responsible for the condition of my body.
>
> I take responsibility for my actions.
>
> I have the power to achieve and maintain my ideal weight.
>
> I have self-discipline and the determination to succeed.
>
> Nothing can stop me from being who I want to be.
>
> My spirit is stronger than anything that can happen to it.
>
> I am in control of my life and my destiny.

Step 3

I know who I am and who I want to become.

I have a clear desire-image of the body I want to have.

> I am firmly committed to achieving my desires.
>
> I control my power through desire and decision.
>
> My desire and decision pave the way for action.

Each day I acknowledge and affirm my desires.

I am committed to living the kind of life I want to live.

Commitment makes it easy to achieve my desires.

I have faith and determination.

I make decisions quickly and easily.

It is only a matter of time before my desire is mine.

I am filled with a sense of joy, accomplishment and strength.

Step 4

I focus my attention on my desire, intent, and purpose.

I dwell with gratitude upon my blessings.

I gratefully acknowledge my talents and my self-worth.

I gratefully acknowledge my physical health and beauty.

I focus on constructive activities that give me joy.

I release my attention from worry, doubt and fear.

I refuse to give my power to obstacles in my way.

My motivation to succeed is increasing everyday.

I am free of the fear of failure.

I am free of the fear of success.

I am successful at whatever I do.

Step 5

I trust the power and wisdom of my subconscious mind.

I listen to my internal guidance from moment to moment.

> My subconscious mind is guiding me toward my desires.
>
> My body heals itself without my conscious effort.
>
> I listen to the inner wisdom of my body.
>
> My inner wisdom tells me when I am hungry.
>
> My inner wisdom tells me what I should eat and how much.
>
> I trust my intuitive impulses to act.
>
> I act on my intuitive impulses to act.
>
> I can achieve my ideal weight without dieting.
>
> I maintain my ideal weight without conscious effort.

Step 6

I love, forgive and accept myself as I am.

I love and accept my body as it is in this moment.

> I deserve an abundance of love and joy in my life.
>
> I willingly give love and receive love.
>
> I gladly give my body what it needs for optimum health.

My body deserves the loving attention I give
it everyday.

I am forgiven for any wrong I have done to others.

I am free of guilt because I am forgiven.

I radiate love and forgiveness to others.

I am truly grateful for my blessings.

I treat myself with respect and dignity.

I am my own best friend.

Step 7

I can imagine what it feels like to possess my desire.

I act "as if" it is mine right now.

I know what it feels like to achieve my ideal weight.

I feel the joy of success and peace of mind.

I have every quality that I need to achieve my ideal
weight.

I have every quality that I need to maintain my ideal
weight.

I feel my new self-image growing stronger everyday.

I am now the person I have always wanted to be.

I have no need to look back; I choose to go forward.

I choose to live my life in the present moment.

I am successful—one day at a time.

Step 8

I take action on every level of my ability to act.

I take action with my imagination and emotions.

I take action with my body.

> I truly desire to achieve my ideal weight.
>
> My mind, my emotions, and my body are aligned with my desire.
>
> I am ready and willing to achieve my ideal weight.
>
> I am firmly committed to having a more slender, healthy body.
>
> I am willing to do what it takes to have a more slender, healthy body.
>
> I am now free of conflicting desires.
>
> I am free of internal conflict and confusion.
>
> I experience inner harmony and peace of mind.
>
> I choose to focus my attention on my purpose and desire.
>
> I am filled with enthusiasm for attaining my desire.
>
> Every action I take brings me closer to my goal.

Affirmations to Release Self-limiting, Self-critical Beliefs

My beliefs, thoughts and feelings are not a permanent part of me.

I instantly recognize all limiting beliefs about myself and my body.

I instantly release self-limiting, self-critical beliefs.

I discard all false, self-critical beliefs like used and worn-out clothing.

I replace self-limiting beliefs with new beliefs that empower and inspire me.

I focus on my strengths and positive attributes.

I choose my thoughts wisely, selecting only those that agree with my new self-image.

Every day in every way, my life is getting better.

My beliefs now bring me the results I want.

Chapter 17

Constructive Actions:
Do's and Don'ts

DO: *Ask Yourself Why You Want To Lose Weight.*

Is your desire to lose weight truly *your* desire? Does it come from cultural or peer pressure to be thin, or do you want to feel and look different for you?

Does your desire to lose weight conflict with other desires you have (such as a desire to fill yourself with more food than your body needs)? If you have conflicting goals, you must choose one or the other, or stand the risk of achieving neither. Question your beliefs in this area. Find out if you are truly willing to change who you are in order to have a more slender body.

DO: *Design Your Own Body Improvement Program.*

You must be the one to design your own body improvement program. Make a list of all the ways in which you would *like* to re-shape and re-make your body's image. Then pick and choose from your list. You may need to exercise, eat light meals in the evening, drink more water, cut out sugar, alcohol or soft drinks, buy new clothes, change jobs, take up an active sport. . .. No one knows but you!

You are the expert authority on yourself. If you have read and studied the latest opinions about weight loss or the benefits of good nutrition and exercise, so much the better. But take the advice of others only when it feels right for you. Adapt it to your own circumstances, needs and desires, and develop a unique plan of action for achieving your ideal weight.

DO: *Allow Yourself To Eat The Foods You Enjoy In Moderation.*

Whatever you try to resist will persist. If you try to resist your favorite foods, you will find yourself thinking of them more than you need to. (You will envision them, see yourself indulging in them, or dwell upon the fear of their power over you.) So allow yourself to eat your favorite foods in moderation.

You may even want to over-indulge in your favorite "fattening" foods, eating only bread or only chocolate for a day. This will take away the power they have over you, and leave you with a stronger desire for fruit and vegetables.

DO: *Eat Like a Fish In The Sea.*

Nibble all day if you want to instead of eating large meals in one sitting. Be like a fish in the sea, swimming in a bountiful environment: they select from this abundance only what they need, when they need it.

DO: *Use Your Willpower The Right Way.*

Use your willpower not to avoid your favorite foods, but to turn your attention toward constructive activities that will increase your self-esteem. Use your willpower to stop the constant barrage of self-critical thoughts and to direct your thoughts and feelings toward self-acceptance and self-praise. Use your willpower to keep your thoughts focused upon your desires, not upon the obstacles that stand in your way.

DO: *Set A Reasonable Goal For Yourself.*

Don't go for the impossible: "I want to lose 20 pounds in one week." Instead of focusing on the goal, focus on your plan for attaining it. Concentrate on what you are doing right now, and the end result will take care of itself.

DO: *Cultivate Non-food Rewards.*

Have non-food payoffs for yourself. Find non-food ways to pamper yourself, such as a manicure, a massage or a new outfit. Motivation is the main thing you need to generate. You can lose your motivation unless you applaud and reward your own progress.

DO: *Use Common Sense.*

Drink more water than you do other liquids; eat high-fiber, natural foods; eat light meals in the evening, heavier meals in the morning (at least for a while); stop eating before or as soon as you are full; eat only when you are hungry, then only as much as you need to satisfy your hunger.

Choose a form of exercise, sport, dance or other activity you enjoy and make a commitment to yourself and your body to engage in it on a regular basis. Provide an outlet for the energy of your body to be expended and released through joyful, invigorating and yet relaxing activities.

DO: *Recognize Self-limiting Beliefs.*

Monitor your thoughts and feelings. Watch as they become triggered by external or stress-related cues instead of internal messages that your body is hungry. Try to determine which beliefs are responsible for any thoughts you might have of limitation and lack. Question your predominant emotions, and they will lead you to the belief that underlies your problem. (For instance, "Why do I feel so discouraged and depressed?")

DO: *Break Up Old Habits.*

Break up old patterns of behavior and habits. If you normally eat standing up, sit down. If you eat sitting down, stand up. If you eat when you watch television, turn it off and stop watching it. If you always start the day by reading the newspaper with a cup of coffee, start the day with an uplifting book and some music, stretching exercises, or a brisk walk.

Take up knitting, join a club, take a class, or a sailing lesson, but do something different to get out of your rut! Habits are most easily changed by replacing them with things you enjoy doing or have always wanted to do but have never had the time. At least for a while, it's extremely important that you don't follow the same routines.

DO: *Find What Gives You The Most Joy.*

There are only so many hours in the day. Make it your goal to be so busy doing things you love to do that you don't have the time to think about food or the desire to overeat. Fill your days with enjoyable activities. Fight boredom, loneliness, fatigue or a stressful job. Take control and initiate constructive change in your life. Choose forward action instead of allowing yourself to merely re-act or be acted upon. Start each day by asking yourself what would give you the greatest joy if you were to do it. Then do it!

DO: *Throw Away The Bathroom Scale.*

If you have a bathroom scale you are fond of using frequently, give it away to a very thin friend or throw it away. And never, ever spend another minute of your time pondering the absurdity (or audacity) of a scale's reading that refuses to budge even though you have starved yourself for days.

What difference does it make whether you weigh 150 pounds or 200 pounds if you are unhappy with the way you look? When you look to a scale for feedback, for approval or disapproval, you hinder your progress toward achieving and maintaining your ideal weight. Each time you jump on a scale eagerly, anxiously awaiting the "good" or "bad" news, you engage your mind and emotions in a silly game that will keep you precisely where you don't want to be.

This kind of behavior isn't at all typical of who you want to become or how you want to live! You want to be free of fear and doubt. You want to trust your mind, emotions and body to spontaneously maintain your ideal weight, so start trusting right now. Face your fear that you can't maintain your weight without a scale, because a scale will never tell you when you have reached your ideal weight and body mass. You must get in touch with an inner sense of your ideal weight and trust this inner sense to maintain it. This inner concept of body-weight is what counts, not a number on the bathroom scale.

Your weight fluctuates constantly, from morning to night, from one week to the next. You haven't won the battle of the bulge until you've won the right to be whatever weight you happen to be in any moment. When you allow a "bad" number on the scale to be the indicator of whether or not you're okay for the day, you've just lost the battle. Your choice is to accept defeat and go on eating or muster more strength to keep on fighting. Give it up, refuse to play the game, and congratulate yourself for winning a major battle!

DO: *Clean Out Your Closets.*

Clean out your closets, throw away old clothes, give away the small sizes that you have been hoping to fit into "someday." This will work wonders for creating a vacuum in your life to be filled with better things. It is also an act of faith that you live in a universe that willingly provides you with everything you need. There is no need to horde, save or hold on to the past. Let it go!

DO: *Give Your Self-Image a Boost.*

Change your hairstyle, your make-up, or buy yourself new shoes and clothes. Dress differently than you presently do. Stop hiding your body. Wear shorts and show a little skin.

DO: *Give Your Self-Confidence a Boost.*

Acquire a new skill, take a class (especially in public speaking), set yourself a task and accomplish it, however small. Learning something new can be very gratifying, giving you a feeling of forward movement and advancement. Set yourself a goal and be determined to achieve it. Success breeds success. You might also want to give yourself an emotional uplift by reading inspirational books (especially autobiographies of individuals who have accomplished great things) or watching inspirational movies.

DO: *Relax and Release All Feelings of Guilt, Anxiety and Frustration.*

Let go of the problem in order to allow solutions to come into your life. Stop trying to analyze all the reasons why you have repeatedly failed to create or maintain your ideal body weight. Replace these thoughts with faith that your inner self will guide you toward success.

DO: *Be Persistent.*

Persistence is one of the greatest secrets of success in achieving your desire. When you refuse to give up, you cannot possibly fail. Remember, there is no such thing as failure—you can only stop trying.

DO: *Cultivate Patience.*

Nature never hurries. Flowers seek sunlight and bees seek nectar, yet neither demand these from nature. Relax with confident expectation that you are receiving your desire for a more slender body. In reality, just as soon as you conceive of yourself as a slender person, you *are* that person in your mind's imagination. You have only to experience it on the physical level, which is simply a matter of time.

DO: *Take One Day At a Time.*

Keep your mind focused in the present. Instead of dwelling on how far you must travel, relax and enjoy your journey. Look at the problem areas objectively and act right now to change these one by one, one day at a time. Each successful day leads to a lifetime of success. "A journey of a thousand miles begins with a single step."

DO: *Practice Absolute Faith.*

Pretend that some higher authority you completely trust (if not your own inner self) has just informed you that you will succeed in achieving and maintaining your ideal weight. How do you feel now? This is the feeling that will rapidly bring about your desire.

DO: *Use Affirmations To Build Your Faith.*

You constantly hypnotize yourself with suggestions, so why not give yourself a new set of them? Step aside and view your thoughts, negative suggestions, and programmed attitudes as separate from you. Write them down, then re-phrase each one of them into a thought that supports and affirms who you want to be and what you want to look like. Repeat these ideas as often as you can in order to build your faith in them.

DO: *Confidently Expect To Be Victorious.*

Use your imagination and emotions to build your expectation of success. Imagine your friends and family com-plementing and congratulating you for achieving your goal of a slender, healthy body. As you experience your victory in your imagination, you build confidence in your ability to reach your goals. Feel the difference between who you are today and who you desire to be; then let that image go and turn your thoughts toward other things that interest you and make you feel successful.

DO: *Write a Script For Your Life and Act It Out.*

Write a script for your life and play-act. If you are truly theatrical, wear a hat or a wig for a day. Visualize yourself as you want to appear and start thinking, talking and acting like the ideal person you want to become. As you think and act like a thin person does, you will know what it's like to live as that person. Thin people don't discuss, think or fret about food and fat at all.

DO: *Trust Your Inner Self To Guide You.*

There may not be a quick solution to weight loss, but there is a lasting one. Abandon your conscious struggle with excess weight and learn to trust the intuitive inner voices within you. Your inner self has the wisdom to guide you toward your ideal weight. Ask for this guidance and then follow your spontaneous impulses toward action. Develop the habit of listening for inner messages of hunger instead of eating in response to emotional need or outer circumstances.

DO: *Praise Yourself.*

Instead of observing how far you have to go, praise yourself for how far you have come. Instead of noticing that your cup is half-empty, realize that it's also half-full. Plants, animals, children and all living things thrive on praise. Try some on yourself and watch it work miracles.

DO: *Accept Yourself "As Is."*

Accept yourself just the way you are, several stomach rolls and all. Accept your present condition, but do not dwell upon it. When you accept who you are and what you are in the present moment, it frees your mind to concentrate on and perceive those qualities that you want to increase. Accept and love yourself for being who you are right now, and you will be ready to give yourself what you truly desire to experience.

DO: *Act Now!*

Act now to apply the knowledge you have, because now is the only moment in which you have power to act. The future is only a series of "now" moments just like today. As you take action, you build confidence and form new habits of behavior that will eventually become second nature to you. If you think you have to struggle, work hard or suffer in order to achieve your desire, you will project it into the imaginary future, thinking there is something you must do or become before you can rightly accept it as your own. Being the person you want to be is something you can do right now.

* * * * *

DON'T: *Go On a Diet.*

Diets don't work. In fact, there is much evidence to suggest that "dieting behavior" actually reinforces your problem with food, keeping you enslaved to the weight-loss weight-gain syndrome. So stop dieting unless you want to diet. It is an unnatural way of thinking about food, and very ineffective in the long run unless you wish to be on a diet for the rest of your life. You can do better things with your time, talent and energy.

DON'T: *Call Yourself "Fat."*

Every time you speak, you transform mental and emotional energy into a more physical-material form. There is energy and power in the spoken word, so stop calling yourself "fat"! Stop talking about food, fat, failure and dieting with your friends, mate or relatives. Make a commitment to stop the incessant, non-constructive inner dialogue about food, dieting, fat, and previous failures. Decide right now that you will never again speak of yourself or the appearance of your body in a degrading, self-critical way.

DON'T: *Dwell On Your Problems.*

When you concentrate on a problem, you perpetuate and reinforce it in your life. You may want to lose weight so badly that you fear you won't be able to. Dwelling on the problem and thus generating fear, puts your power in reverse and causes you to create what you don't want! Concentrate on having what you want instead of fearing that you never will.

[handwritten annotation: A.M. Dr Joy - Let it go! Radio]

DON'T: *Discuss Your Success (or Plans For Success) With Others.*

Never discuss your desire for a slender body, your dieting success or failures, or anything at all related to the "problem" with friends and family. This chatter only serves to reinforce the image of yourself as a "fat" person with a weight "problem," in your mind and theirs.

Too much talk also dissipates your energy for action and subjects your desire to cross-currents from others who do not share your enthusiasm for success. Often, others want you to remain the way you are because it reinforces their own mistaken beliefs in their lack of power. Or your failures may make them feel more powerful because you are so miserable.

In either case, beware. Keep your plans for success and happiness to yourself, and let your new image speak for itself.

DON'T: *Criticize Yourself.*

Don't criticize yourself for every tiny physical flaw or "negative" character trait. Don't criticize and berate yourself for your failures or your excess fat. Stop questioning why you have failed in the past, and praise yourself for at least trying. Never attempt to control your eating habits with self-criticism, fear, anxiety and threats—this won't work!

You will realize the vision of your dominant thoughts. Therefore, focus upon your strengths, not your weaknesses, and these will be increased.

DON'T: *Compare Yourself To Others.*

Never make the mistake of comparing yourself or your body with someone else. To compare your own unique talents and attributes with someone else's is truly an exercise in futility. There will always be someone who appears to be happier, more talented, or more beautiful than you are.

If you must compare yourself to someone, compare yourself to your own ideal image of yourself and your body. If you have a picture of yourself at your desired weight, use this as your source of inspiration, and stop gazing at photos of others wishing you could be like them. Each of us is here for a different purpose. And that purpose has nothing to do with duplicating the looks and personality of anyone else.

DON'T: *Give Power To Past Mistakes.*

"What is," "what could have been," and "what can be" are not worlds apart, they are thoughts and feelings apart. They are the mental effort it takes to decide once and for all that you will not be controlled by faulty beliefs or misguided fears that you have somehow failed to do what you "should" have done.

You have access to the same number of hours in the day and the same incredible power that others are using right now to live their lives as they choose. You have the power to transform your life as you choose.

DON'T: *Buy Foods That You Can't Resist.*

Don't buy any foods that you are unable to resist. Have someone else do the shopping for you or make a list of what you want to buy and stick to it. Out of sight is out of mind *and* out of mouth.

DON'T: *Worry About How Or When You Will Lose Weight.*

Worrying is worthless activity. If you catch yourself worrying about how or when you will lose weight, read the 8 Steps until you have calmed your fears. Turn your worry into constructive activity by designing a plan of action that inspires and empowers you. Then make a commitment to follow through with your plan. Take action right away and trust that you will succeed in time. Worrying won't make it happen any faster, but trusting and persisting with constructive action will.

DON'T: *Set Strict Or Unreasonable Time Limits On Achieving Your Desire.*

Stop setting unreasonable deadlines on your goal to achieve weight loss. You didn't arrive at your current mental-emotional-physical state all at once, so don't expect to achieve a new one all at once. If you fail to meet your goal within a given time frame, you may think you've lost control and start judging and criticizing yourself. This adds to the anxiety you experience—but not to your success. The weight you gained didn't happen overnight and neither will the weight you lose.

DON'T: *Search For Answers Outside Yourself.*

The answer to your problem lies within you, within your mind, within your emotions, and within your unique body chemistry. The answers will come when you open your mind, ask different questions, and expect to get answers. The answers will come with your willingness to see your self, your body and your life from a new perspective; with your desire, decision and determination to succeed.

DON'T: *Watch Or Wait For Your Desire To Come About.*

Looking for evidence of a change in your body is an expression of doubt. You will not see instantaneous change, but instead wake up one day and realize you are there! You don't see yourself growing from a child to an adult; nor do you see a flower blossom overnight. If you were to try to watch these processes, it would seem to take an eternity.

DON'T: *Make This Complicated!*

Keep it simple and don't over-analyze these principles. It is actually a very simple, natural process that will unfold as you ask it to. You do not have to follow any particular technique to the letter; you are using these principles every day of your life. Think about how you succeed in other endeavors (something as simple as planning a vacation) and you will know that you have what it takes to achieve your desire.

JUST DO IT!

Each day of your life is a new beginning
and the journey never really ends.

Bon Voyage!

Glossary of Power Words

What the mind can conceive and believe, the mind can achieve.

--Napolean Hill

Glossary of Power Words

Accept: To receive or willingly take what is offered or given. To *believe* in; to regard as normal or inevitable. *Synonyms:* receive, take, affirm, acknowledge.

Believe / Belief: Conviction or acceptance that certain things are true or real. To believe is to *accept* something as truth. *Synonyms: faith*, confidence, *trust*, conviction, feeling intuition, *expectation*, judgment, also opinion or theory.

Commit / Commitment: A pledge or promise to do something. *Synonyms:* pledge, promise, *decision*.

Decide / Decision: The act of making up one's mind; determination; firmness of mind. Free from ambiguity and hesitation, beyond a doubt; a disposition to prompt *action*; to make a choice; a result arrived at after consideration. *Synonyms*: conclusion, determination, will, choice.

Desire: To wish or long for; to ask for, request. A conscious impulse toward an object or experience that promises enjoyment or satisfaction in its attainment. *Synonyms:* need, want, longing, aspiration, ambition, ask.

Emotion / Feelings: Any of various complex reactions with both mental and physical manifestations, as love, hate, fear, anger; experienced as strong feeling and involving physiological changes that prepare the body for *action*. *Synonyms:* love, sympathy, mental conflict, worry, jealousy, fear, sadness, despair, anger, joy, happiness.

Expect / Expectation: To expect is to look forward to the occurrence of something, to wait for, anticipate, to consider probable or certain. *Synonyms:* anticipation; *trust*, confidence, anticipatory *desire*.

Faith: A firm *belief* in something for which there is no proof. A calm assurance and an inner knowingness that the right thing is being accomplished. *Synonyms: belief, trust,* acceptance, confident *expectation.*

Forgive: To give up resentment against or the desire to punish; stop being angry with. *Synonyms:* excuse, overlook.

Imagine / Imagination: The act or power of forming a mental image of something not present to the senses; creative ability, a creation of the mind: creative power, envisioning the past as present. *Synonyms:* mental image, *thought,* dream, envision, conceive, originate, invent, picture to oneself.

Love: A deep and tender feeling of affection for or devotion to a person or persons. To take joy in, care for, appreciate. *Synonyms:* passionate affection, cherish, admire, prize, esteem.

Think / Thought: The action or process of thinking, the power to *imagine;* serious consideration, recollection, reasoning power. *Synonyms:* stream of consciousness, self-consultation, meditation, reflection, contemplation, introspection, idea, opinion, *belief, view, imagination.*

Trust: A firm *belief* or confidence in the honesty, integrity, reliability of another person or thing. *Synonyms: belief,* confident *expectation,* conviction, *faith.*

Definitions have been revised from
WEBSTER'S NEW WORLD DICTIONARY,
SECOND COLLEGE EDITION